God Magnified, Part 6

Appraising the Most High

I0200393

By Eric Mumford

LIFECHANGERS®

P.O. Box 3709 ❖ Cookeville, TN 38502
931.520.3730 ❖ lc@lifechangers.org

The Scripture quotations contained in this book are from:
The New American Standard Bible®, Copyright © 1960, 1962, 1963, 1971, 1972, 1973, 1975, 1977, 1995 by The Lockman Foundation.

PLUMBLINE

Published by:

LIFECHANGERS ®
LIBRARY SERIES

P.O. Box 3709 | Cookeville, TN 38502
(800) 521-5676 | www.lifechangers.org

All Rights Reserved
ISBN 978-1-940054-02-5

© 2014 Lifechangers
All Rights Reserved
Printed in the United States of America

Contents

God Magnified Statements
14 Pillars of the Trinity's Dwelling Place

Pillar 1 | God is an "**Us**"– three Individuals (Gen. 1:26, 3:22, 11:7; Isa. 6:8).

Pillar 2 | "God is **one**" (Deut. 6:4; Mark 12:29).

Pillar 3 | "God is **love (*Agape*)**" (1 John 4:8, 16).

Pillar 4 | "God is a **sun**" (Psa. 84:11).

Pillar 5 | "**Holy, Holy, Holy** is the Lord God, the Almighty" (Rev. 4:8; Isa. 6:3).

Pillar 6 | "God is **Light**" (1 John 1:5).

Pillar 7 | "The eternal God is a **dwelling place**" (Deut. 33:27).

Pillar 8 | "God **in Christ**" (Col. 2:9; 2 Cor. 5:19; Eph. 4:32).

Pillar 9 | "God is **spirit**" (John 4:24).

Pillar 10 | "God is **true**" (John 3:33).

Pillar 11 | "The Lord is a God of **justice**" (Isa. 30:18).

Pillar 12 | "The Lord, whose name is *Jealous*, is a **jealous** God" (Ex. 34:14).

Pillar 13 | "God is a **consuming fire**" (Deut. 4:24; Heb. 12:29).

Pillar 14 | God is three sacrificial **Self-sharers**.

God Magnified, Part 6
Appraising the Most High

by Eric Mumford

Introduction

In this *Plumbline* series, we are discovering the "**dwelling place**" which the Persons of the Trinity not only *share* but which the three Eternals *are*. Before the heavens and the earth or any created being existed, the "Eternal **Father**" (Isa. 9:6), the "eternal **Son**" (1 Tim. 1:16-17; John 1:1), and the "eternal **Spirit**" (Heb. 9:14), *Themselves*, constituted "the **eternal kingdom**" (2 Pet. 1:11). God is three relational, Self-giving Persons who *mutually indwell* One Another. The Triune-God is profoundly inclusive and hospitable; into this relational, inter-Personal infrastructure, known as the kingdom of God, we have been invited. The Triune-God is calling us Home into Themselves: *re-gene-rating*, fusing, and acculturating us as adopted children into **God in Christ**.

The *God Is* or God Magnified statements of the Scriptures are like pillars of a covered porch built around the entire circumference of **God is a dwelling place**; each pillar serves as a lens to see and understand the next truth about God. Progressive magnification of these *God is* declarations leads to a three-dimensional understanding of the eternal kingdom and draws us to enter and participate through the God-Man Jesus in the *eternal life* of the Triune-God. As kingdom emigrants, we are pioneering forward together into this unfolding revelation of **the fusion of the Trinity**.

In the previous volume, *God Magnified Part 5, Discerning the Truth*, we magnified "God is true" (John 3:33). We discovered why "truth is in Jesus" (Eph. 4:21), and by His grace, we are becoming sharers in Paul's testimony that **"the truth of Christ is in me"** (2 Cor. 11:10). Jesus testified that, "God is spirit and those who worship Him must worship **in spirit** [*prevailing, life-giving human spirit*] and **truth** [*fuse-able DNA of Agape*]" (John 4:24). We carefully examined this truth, which the Triune-God desires to plant, cultivate, and mature within us so that we may participate in a relationship of reciprocal *generosity* with Father, Son, Spirit, and one another—the kingdom of God.

We learned that the love (*Agape*) of the Father, Son, and Spirit for One another and for us is **true**; it is **"unchanging love"** (Micah 7:18). God is true because "God is faithful" (1 Cor. 1:9); "He swears to His own hurt and does not change" (Psa. 15:4). Paul wrote, "Let *Agape* be **without hypocrisy**" (Rom. 12:9). In contrast to true Love, we examined *eros*—a treacherous, **counterfeit self-love**, which the Scriptures call **"the lie"** (John 8:44; Rom. 3:7). We also gained a better understanding of *Agape* and *eros* through the secular terms *altruism* and *egoism*. Since "*Agape* never fails" (1 Cor. 13:8), the always-true Love of the Triune-God won't let you down, rather, it picks you up when you fall. More precisely, Father, Son, and Spirit *are* a kind of love that affords each of us the **freedom to fall**—to *choose* "the lie" and *persist* in it but through repentance sacrificially lifts us up again in **resurrection**.

Now, in *God Magnified Part Six: Appraising the Most High*, we will discover why Father, Son, and Spirit, together, are "the Most High God" (Psa. 78:35; Heb. 7:1) and see how mankind *fell* out of the relational, interpersonal life of the Triune-God by *buying into* the lie, *de-gene-rating* in self-worthship, becoming acculturated into Worthless's [literal meaning of Satan] world economy, and therefore, existing in an **eclipse** from God Most High.

In the next volume, *God Magnified Part Seven: Surveying the Economy of the Kingdom*, we will see how "Jesus, Son of the Most High God," (Luke 8:28) came down to us in our fallen state to mentor us in **kingdom economics** that we might become "**sons** [*and daughters*] **of the Most High**" (Luke 6:35).

The Man Upstairs

In everyday language, such as we hear in the lyrics of country music, God is often referred to as "**the Man upstairs**." But *why* is God upstairs? What exactly are we supposed to understand about God from the fact that He is "on high" (Luke 1:78; Heb. 1:3)? Most human beings are suspicious of God in varying degrees, all of us intentionally "suppress the truth" (Rom. 1:18) of God in one way or another, and some even attempt to deny the existence of God altogether; yet, every human being *intuitively knows* that our Creator is up there "because that which is known about God is **evident within them**, for God made it evident to them" (Rom. 1:19). When desperate circumstances confront a man and force him to acknowledge his own extremity, he will literally raise his eyes upward to God. But how do most of us see "the Man upstairs" on all the other *regular* days?

As *de-gene-rate* captives of "**the lie**" [**self-love, self-worth-ship**] (John 8:44), we are naturally predisposed to misunderstand *why* God is upstairs. Both consciously and unconsciously, we envision an **aloof, condescending judge**—an autonomous, self-righteous critic who looks down His nose at us from a lofty distance. Some see a **self-sufficient Father figure** who is always right, always disappointed, and impossible to please. In the parable of the talents, Jesus exposed our suspicious estimation of God: "Master, I knew you to be a **hard man** [*a calculative taker*] reaping where you did not sow and gathering where you scattered no seed [*exacting from others for your own self-interest*]" (Matt. 25:24).

We characterize God according to the darkness of the self-worth-ship or **individual-ism** that is within us. Therefore, in self-preservation, we choose to maintain our own safe distance from God by simply marginalizing and ignoring Him. We have learned to suppress the truth of God *within* us by "drinking old wine" (Luke 5:39)—living in a perpetually inebriated state of self-indulgence and self-absorption in order that our old, familiar, **alternate reality** (unreality), in which *self* is essentially *god* and *master*, might remain undisturbed.

In this intoxicated condition, however, it is so easy to overlook the fact that the Man upstairs is *not* a solitary Being at all, rather **God is an "Us"** (Gen. 1:26; Isa. 6:8). Self-focus has effectively eclipsed us from true Reality: God is not a *solitary*, stoic elitist but rather **three humble, purely relational Individuals** fused in such profound Oneness that the Scriptures refer to all three, together, as a "He"—"I AM WHO I AM" (Ex. 3:14)! The Spirit of God has come to "sober" us up from self-magnification (see 1 Cor. 15:34; 1 Pet. 1:13) and to teach us how to magnify "God in Christ." Exposure to the Light of this knowledge prepares our spirit and renews our mind to comprehend *why* the eternal Trinity is "**God Most High**" (Gen. 14:18; Psa. 57:2; Dan. 3:26; Acts 16:17; Heb. 7:1).

It is certainly true that God the *Father*, God the *Son*, and God the *Holy Spirit* are distinguished from all created beings as *uncreated* Eternals. However, consider with me that God is also *Most High* because **Father, Son, and Spirit exalt One Another**. God is "Holy, Holy, Holy:" three, *eros*-free (self-less) Individuals who dwell in "the fullness" of sacrificial Self-giving *to* One Another. This is known as *perichoresis*: mutual indwelling and interpenetration without loss of personal identity. Moses referred to God's house as "the highest heaven" [*lit. Heb.: heaven of heavens*] (Deut. 10:14), then he made it clear that "the eternal God *is* a dwelling place" (Deut. 33:27).

The dynamic activity of this relational, inter-Personal Oneness is **mutual exaltation**. As Individuals, Father, Son, and Spirit perpetually cherish, glorify, and exalt *One Another* and never *their individual Selves*. The outcome is that these Three, together as One God, are glorified, exalted, and **elevated**! These three sacrificial Self-sharers are *all-true* to One Another in *Agape*; therefore, the Triune-God is "Most High." Father, Son, and Spirit **carry One Another up the stairs**; therefore, God is the Man upstairs.

The presupposition of all religion and philosophy is the futile idea (the lie) that an individual, by self-effort, can climb these stairs. However, the fact is, no human being can climb these stairs; one must be **carried up** (see Ezek. 8:3; Luke 24:51; 2 Cor. 12:2; 1 Thes. 4:17; Rev. 21:10). Our Triune-God intends to teach us how to carry one another up these stairs.

"The Most High" is certainly God's *permanent* office, but the Scriptures reveal it is more—a *dynamic*, relational life. Isaiah saw "Holy, Holy, Holy," the All-Three-Mighty, and wrote: "I saw the Lord sitting on a throne, lofty and exalted…. **Seraphim** [*created angelic beings*] **stood above Him**" (Isa. 6:1-3). Clearly, this lofty and exalted place is *not* simply a positional, spatial reality since the Triune-God is content for angels to stand *above* Him. As natural-minded men acculturated in the *eros* rationale, we tend to think of *the Most High* as one, solitary **king of the mountain** who uses force to keep everyone beneath Him, but this could not be further from the truth. "God Most High" is a *relational* reality of mutual exaltation that *cannot* be accurately understood from man's corrupt paradigm of **hierarchy**: the distinction of rank preserved.

Why God Is Worthy

Eight hundred years after the time of Isaiah, John saw "Holy, Holy, Holy," and he heard the inhabitants of heaven saying, "**Worthy** are You, our Lord and our God [*Three "true" to One Another and to us*], to receive glory and honor and power" (Rev. 4:8-11). God is worthy; *de-gene-rate* human beings are **unworthy**. Our nature, **corrupted** by "the lie" of self-worth-ship moves us to **compete** for honor and recognition, to "be seen by men" (Matt. 6:5). As individualists, we instinctively **contend** for the power to exalt, gratify, and preserve ourselves, as well as the means to control, judge, and exploit others. As the Spirit helps us to see things clearly, we discover that this very toxic motivation—seeking **fortune and glory** for self—controls the behavior of ordinary people like us in everyday life.

To understand why "God is worthy," we must examine how these three incorruptible Eternals handle "power and **riches and** wisdom and might and honor and glory and blessing" (Rev. 5:12). Father, Son, and Spirit are true and speak truth because each never speaks of Himself in self-reference or self-promotion; He only speaks of the other Two. **Father** does not speak of Himself, but only of His "beloved Son" in whom He is "well-pleased" (Matt. 3:17; 17:5) and of the Spirit of His Son whom He "has sent into our hearts crying, 'Abba! Father!'" (Gal. 4:6). The **Son** does not speak of Himself: "If I glorify Myself, My glory is nothing [worthless]; it is My Father who glorifies Me" (John 8:54). He came to reveal the Father and the Spirit of His Father. The **Spirit** does not speak from Himself, but reveals the Father and the Son:

> [26]*When the Helper comes, whom I will send to you from the Father, that is the **Spirit of truth** who proceeds from the Father [not from Himself], He will **testify about Me** [the Nucleus: God in Christ].... [13]But when He, the Spirit of truth [Agape], comes, He will **guide you into all the truth** [relational, inter-personal Oneness]; for He will not speak on His own initiative [eros self-reference], but whatever He hears, He will speak.... [14]He will glorify Me, for He will **take of Mine** [the "fullness" of the kingdom] **and disclose it to you** [Nucleus-giving Love] (John 15:26; 16:13-14).*

The Apostle John saw into this dynamic, Self-sharing life of the Triune-Most High occurring within the Nucleus of Jesus, and he bought into that life so comprehensively that in his own gospel he would not reference himself by his own name, but only as "the disciple whom Jesus loved" (John 21:20). Curiously, *The Gospel of John* is the most well-read book in the Bible and the Bible is the most widely circulated book in all literary history!

The Trinity not only *share* all honor and glory and blessing by mutual glorification, They also *share* all power, authority, and judgment. Jesus testified:

> [35] *The Father loves the Son [Father is true in Agape] and has given all things into His hand....*
>
> [20] *and shows Him all things that He Himself is doing....* [22] *For* **not even the Father judges anyone, but He has given all judgment to the Son.**... [30] *I can do nothing on My own initiative [autonomously]. As I hear I judge; and My judgment is just [true in Agape], because* **I do not seek My own will** *[self-will], but the will of Him who sent Me.* [31] *If I alone [autonomously] testify of Myself [self-reference] My testimony is* **not true** *[eros–"the lie"].* [32] *There is another who testifies of Me, and I know that the testimony He gives about Me is* **true** *["the fullness" of the Trinity dwells within Me to be revealed*

through Me]…. ³⁴But the testimony which I
receive is not from man, but I say these things
so that you may be saved [fused into Me—the
God-Man Nucleus] (John 3:35; 5:20, 22,
30, 32, 34).

Jesus added, "All things have been handed over to
Me by My Father" (Luke 10:22). The Son, however,
does not act as a **proprietor** but as a "Servant" (Isa.
42:1) or **Steward** of the kingdom; the Son is eagerly
awaiting "the end" when He can joyfully "hand
over the kingdom [*back*] to God the Father" (1 Cor.
15:24). In the meantime, the Son is at Father's right
hand, and all authority was handed over by the Father
and Son to the Holy Spirit whom They sent to *re-
gene-rate*, fuse, and acculturate us into the kingdom of
the combined and combining God-Man Jesus Christ.
None of the Three have ever sought His Own glory or
power; **Each will only *receive* glory and power for
the purpose of *revealing* the other Two** and fulfilling
the kingdom of the fusion Oneness of God and man.

Now *this* kingdom is clearly "not of this world"
(John 18:36). Among men it is said that power
corrupts and absolute power corrupts absolutely,
however, this is entirely untrue of the Omnipotent yet
"incorruptible God" (Rom. 1:23)—three Self-sharers
whose fusion power is stewarded in true Oneness.
George MacDonald observed:

*How terribly, then, have the theologians misrepresented God! Nearly all of them represent Him as a great King [a solitary Being] on a grand throne, **thinking how grand He is** [self-worth-ship], and making it the business of His and the end of His universe to keep up His glory [self-promotion], wielding the thunderbolts of Jupiter against them that take His name in vain [self-defense]. They would not allow this, but follow out what they say, and it comes much to this.... Brothers, have you found our King? There He is [Triune-God in Christ] kissing **little children** and saying they are like God [Three humble, child-like Eternals]...the simplest peasant who loves his children and his sheep were—no, not a truer, for the other is false, but—a **true** type of our God beside that **monstrosity of a monarch*** (MacDonald, *The Child in the Midst*, p. 34).

"The eternal kingdom" (2 Pet. 1:11) is the Trinity *Themselves*: "God *is* a dwelling place" (Deut. 33:27). The kingdom of the Triune-Holy is lifted "**on high**" (Psa. 93:4; Heb. 1:3) by the extreme Self-forsaking and Self-giving way in which Father, Son, and Spirit *relate* to One Another and to us. This "lofty and exalted" dwelling place is **not a manifestation of**

pride and self-exaltation but quite the opposite—this cohabitation is facilitated by the profound **humility** and the child-likeness of each of the three Eternals.

> [15]*For thus says the **high and exalted One** who lives forever [three Eternals fused in incorruptible Love], whose name is Holy [Triune-Holy; one shared name], **"I dwell on a high and holy place** [three eros-free, self-less Eternals mutually indwelling One Another], **and also with the contrite and lowly of spirit** in order to revive the spirit of the lowly and to revive the heart of the contrite [by Our sacrificial Self-giving]....*
> [1]*Heaven is My throne and earth is My footstool. Where then is a **house** you could build for Me? And where is a place that I may **rest** [in relational Oneness, reciprocal gene-rosity]?* [2]*...But to this one I will look [to cohabit with], to him who is **humble** [self-emptied] **and contrite** [fuse-able] **of spirit**, and who trembles at My word [Jesus: God-Man Nucleus]"* (Isa. 57:15; 66:1-2).

Father, Son, and Spirit desire to dwell with the lowly and contrite because They find an affinity with such human beings—a fuse-able DNA-match. Jesus revealed this law to mankind: "Whoever **exalts himself** [eros, self-worth-ship] shall be humbled; and whoever **humbles himself** [Agape, self-emptying] shall be exalted" (Matt. 23:12). When the "Us" created human beings, They did *not* simultaneously create and establish this universal law simply to govern mankind; this *eternal law* originated in the "true" nature of our Triune-Creator *Themselves*. The dynamic movement of the kingdom of God can be described as a **downward ascent** because all the individuals participating in it are continually humbling themselves to exalt one another! The fall of man is a contrary movement—an upward descent.

Pride is rooted in *eros* rationale—**one-dimensional** thinking: *me*. Conversely, **humility** is rooted in *Agape* rationale—**multi-dimensional** thinking: *us*. This self-forgetful, "Us" thinking is "the mind of the Lord...the mind of Christ" (1 Cor. 2:16). This is how it works. From the Son's perspective, the kingdom is "My **Father's** kingdom" (Matt. 26:29). As a Sharer in the exact same Love, the Father's perspective is a bit different: "Father has transferred us to the kingdom of His beloved Son" or the **Son** of His *Agape* [*His Son's kingdom*]" (Col. 1:13). Together, Father and Son share this perspective: "the kingdom of God is righteousness and peace and joy in the **Holy Spirit**" (Rom. 14:17).

Before we continue, allow me to testify of *how* this understanding of God Most High was given to me. I was sharing on "God in Christ" with a group in Oklahoma City for three days and attempting to answer their many insightful questions. Curiously, as we were comparing the *life-giving* **Vortex of the Trinity** and the inverted, *life-taking* dynamic of black holes (kingdom of darkness), we heard sirens blaring outside the facility, warning us that **tornadoes** were touching down in the area. *Naturally*, the timing of this planted the *spiritual* reality of what we were learning deep within each one of us!

Having completed the final session, I returned to the house of my dear friends and stretched out exhausted on their living room carpet. As I lay there, the Triune-God flooded me with *the fullness* of His pleasure that His people were coming to know Him, losing their suspicion of Him, and understanding how to fuse into God in Christ. Through this Presence, the voice of the Lord gripped me in a very direct and intentional way, saying, "Do you know why **I AM God Most High?**" I responded, "I guess not, since You are asking me!" The Lord answered, "**We are Three who exalt One Another**."

This experience was very deep and intimate—a gift of *seeing-into* that "surpasses knowledge" (Eph. 3:19). The name *God Most High* was not among the *God is* statements first revealed to me as porch pillars of the kingdom. As I wept in "the Light of the knowledge of the glory" (2 Cor. 4:6), I felt impressed that God was *delighted* with the way I had been stewarding, cherishing, and sacrificially giving myself to *the measure* of the revelation entrusted to me thus far by carrying it in proclamation. I also perceived how jealously and zealously the Trinity desires for us all to be **made full and complete** (see Col. 2:10; John 17:13) **with increasing fullnesses**—to receive, enter, and participate in greater dimensions of the one reality of the Triune-*Agape* in Christ.

I was immediately reminded of Jesus' parable of the talents: "His master said to him, 'Well done, good and faithful slave. **You were faithful with a few** things, I will put you in charge of many things; **enter into the joy** [*superabundant Triune-fullness*] **of your master**'" (Matt. 25:21). If we will continue to "practice the truth [*Trinity-likeness*]" (John 3:21) together, imagine what is yet to come! "There will be no end to the **increase** of His government or of peace [*the kingdom*]" (Isa. 9:7).

The Fall in Economic Terms

Our Creator is an "**Us**"—three *Self-sharers* who desired to *share* Their superabundant, eternal life of reciprocal *Agape* and mutual exaltation with Their creation. God Most High created us in Their own Self-giving *image* and fuse-able *likeness* in order to **progressively *lift* us into Themselves**. God planted a seed of Their own *gene-rous* nature (*Agape* DNA) within mankind and purposed for it to *mature* "from faith to faith" (Rom. 1:17) and "from life to life" (2 Cor. 2:16) and "from glory to glory" (2 Cor. 3:18).

The Triune-God intentionally set Their entire creation free. Both angels and human beings have their origin in God Most High; each created being was granted their own nucleus of **individuality** and **free will** because relational, inter-personal *fusion* (all-true Love) can only occur between *free* individuals who *freely* reciprocate God's sacrificial Self-giving from a *willing* spirit. These three, uncreated Self-sharers purposed to *share* Their *dwelling place* of Triune-solidarity (the Rock) with created beings by establishing within Themselves "**a kingdom which cannot be shaken**" (Heb. 12:28)—a *cohabitation* of peace in which God, angels, and human beings *willingly* abide in **fusion** with one another by true, reciprocal Love.

However, one third of the angels of God and the first man and woman *abused* this gift and **fell** out of the relational, inter-personal *fusion* dynamic of God Most High. These created beings were **corrupted** by sin—(*eros*) self-love, individualism—therefore they were no longer self-givers, no longer *fuse-able*, no longer fit to cohabit in the Trinity's sacred nest of vulnerable rest. The power of **fission**—free individuals *splintering* from God in self-indulgence, self-will, and self-worship—**shook the heavens** (see Luke 21:26; Heb. 12:27). Fission and fusion cannot abide together in an unshakable kingdom; therefore, these angelic and human individualists not only *fell* out of the Triune-dwelling place, they were "**thrown down**" (Dan. 8:11; Rev. 12:9) and **driven out** (see Gen. 3:24).

In order for us to *rediscover* the transcendent reality of God Most High, it is essential to understand **the fall of man**—how all the offspring of Adam became enslaved in darkness and why the kingdom of God was thereafter **eclipsed** to mankind in secret mystery. Jesus referred to this eclipsed reality as "**the mysteries of the kingdom of heaven**" (Matt. 13:11). Paul called it "the mystery of godliness [*Trinity-like Agape*]" (1 Tim. 3:16); "the **mystery** which for ages has been **hidden in God** who created all things" (Eph. 3:9); and "the **mystery** which has been hidden from the past ages and generations [*fallen de-gene-rates*], but has now been **manifested** to His saints [*lit. holy ones; e.g., children re-gene-rating in the fuse-able DNA of the God-Man Jesus*]" (Col. 1:26).

Both angels and human beings *fell* because "they **exchanged** the glory of God [*sacrificial self-giving– fusion*] for a lie [*lit. the lie; self-love–fission*], and worshipped and served the creature [*self-worth-ship*] rather than the Creator [*true worth-ship*]" (Rom. 1:25). Curiously, as we investigate this mystery, we discover the Scriptures consistently use **economic terms**, such as *exchanged*, to explain the way individuals enter and participate both in the kingdom of God as well as in the kingdom of darkness. The *economy* of "the world" (1 John 2:16) is driven by self-indulgence (*eros*): **buying and selling** one another for calculated personal gain. The *economy* of the kingdom functions by sacrificial self-giving (*Agape*): **giving and receiving** in order to give again—reciprocal gene-rosity. Paul explained:

> [15]*You yourselves also know, Philippians… no church **shared** with me in the matter of **giving and receiving** [reciprocal gene-*

*rosity] but you alone [16]...more than once you sent a gift for my needs. [17]Not that I seek the gift itself [eros], but I seek for the **profit which increases to your account** [Agape]. [18]**But I have received everything in full** and have an **abundance** [the kingdom is superabundant, relational fullness]; I am amply supplied, having received from Epaphroditus what you have sent [Paul received only to give again], a fragrant aroma, an acceptable **sacrifice**, well-pleasing to God [participation in the economy of the Most High]. [19]And my God will **supply** all your needs [material and spiritual] according to His **riches in glory** [superabundant yield of Triune-Agape] in Christ Jesus [the God-Man Nucleus] (Phil. 4:15-19).*

In this corrupt world, we *love things* and use people to get things; in the kingdom, we *love people* and use things to love people. "For all that is in **the world**, the **lust** [*insatiable appetite*] of the flesh [*self-indulgence*] and the **lust** of the eyes [*self-will: i.e. I will have*] and the **boastful pride** of life [*self-worth-ship*], is not from the Father, but is from **the world**" (1 John 2:16).

The economy of *the world* is a **consumer-driven** operation—a counterproductive exercise of takers that results in lack. Our *de-gene-rate* instinct as individualists— self-indulgence, self-preservation, and fear of scarcity and loss—precipitates a **free-fall into famine** and a war-like state in which *predatory* behavior matures. For example, if customers suspect their bank is no longer able to multiply and preserve their money, panic quickly spreads and precipitates a run on the bank. The economy of *the kingdom* is a **producer-driven** operation—a fruit-bearing exercise of givers that **gene-rates superabundant bounty**. Free individuals who participate in the dynamic of *reciprocal gene-rosity* facilitate a cohabitation of peace in which resources are exponentially multiplied and *gene-rous* behavior matures.

Curiously, circumstances of scarcity and famine are the most ideal conditions for this inter-personal dynamic of gene-rative bounty to occur (see Acts 11:28-30; 2 Cor. 8:1-5)! Reporters once asked Mother Teresa why the Sisters of Mercy would remove the carpeting and hot water heaters out of the facilities donated to them for ministry centers. She replied, "It may sound absurd, but the more we have, the less we give...we choose not to have." Paul described how the economy of the kingdom functions:

> *6He who sows sparingly will also reap* ***sparingly*** *[famine], and he who sows bountifully will also reap* ***bountifully*** *[relational fullness].... 8And God [Most High] is able to make all grace abound to you, so that always having all sufficiency in everything, you may have an* ***abundance for every good deed*** *[acts of sacrificial self-*

giving].... *10Now God who **supplies** seed to the sower [giver] and bread for food will supply and **multiply** your seed for sowing and increase the harvest of your righteousness [maturity in gene-rous DNA]; 11you will be **enriched** in everything [natural and spiritual] for all **liberality**, which through us is **producing** thanksgivings to God [reciprocal gene-rosity] (2 Cor. 9:6-11).*

Famine and *bounty* are not simply economic conditions; each is a distinct **rationale** rooted in a **nature** and manifested in **behavior**. Before Jesus fed 5,000 from five loaves and two fish, He confronted this famine mentality in His disciples saying, "They do not need to go away; you give them something to eat!" (Matt. 14:16). Apart from God's magnanimous *gene-rosity*—mercifully feeding a world full of beastly takers—clearly none of us *de-gene-rates* would survive the famines we *ourselves* repeatedly cause on the earth (see Gen. 41:56; Acts 14:16-17).

The economy of the kingdom is an expression of **God's own *gene-rous* nature**, Triune-*Agape*. The entire focus, energy, and life of each Person of the Trinity is exalting and **adding to** the other Two. Father, Son, and Spirit give *all* to One Another and only receive from One Another motivated by an innate desire to give again in **reciprocal gene-rosity**: "Father, glorify Your Son, that I may glorify You" (John 17:1). None of the Three needs to exalt or promote Himself nor buy, sell, trade, or take *for* Himself because the full-time job of the other Two is to glorify Him and give *all* to Him. Since Father, Son, and Spirit do not sell One Another, They cannot be bought with any bribe; therefore, the Triune-Holy is "the **incorruptible** God" (Rom. 1:23).

God creates each human being with both a *soul* (the faculty of free will and desire) and a *spirit*—the faculty by which "one joins [*fuses*] himself to the Lord" (1 Cor. 6:17) and to others. Our Creator designed the dynamic relationship between an individual's soul and spirit as a gift of *fuse-ability*—the innate **freedom and power of faith** to not just believe *in* God but to believe *into* God. Even the demons believe *in* God (see James 2:19); but we are called to **buy into** Him, that is, to join ourselves to the Lord in Trinity-like fusion by volitional, sacrificial self-giving. However, this gift of faith we have received can be used or abused; we are *free* to **buy into** either *Light* or *darkness* (see 1 John 2:8-11). By the free exercise of soul and spirit, an individual can **put his trust into** *the truth* or into *the lie* (see Rom. 3:7).

Both the economy of the kingdom and the economy of the world operate by **exchanges**—an individual must *sell* in order to *buy*. Jesus said, "The kingdom of heaven is like a **treasure** hidden in the field, which **a man found** and hid again; and from joy over it he goes and **sells** all that he has and **buys** that field" (Matt. 13:44). Saul, who became a new creation named Paul, actually made this *exchange* and used economic terms to describe it:

*8I **count** all things to be **loss** [debited] in view of the surpassing **value** of knowing Christ Jesus my Lord, for whom I have suffered the **loss** of all things [e.g., my own life: racial, religious, and vocational identity and achievements], and **count** them but rubbish so that I may **gain Christ** [**fuse into the Nucleus of the Trinity**] (Phil. 3:8).*

King Solomon advised, "**Buy truth and do not sell it**" (Prov. 23:23). However, in his latter days, Solomon himself *sold* the inheritance of truth (rationale and economy of *Agape*) entrusted to him. In *con-fusion* to foreign wives, he used his gift as God's anointed builder to construct temples for their gods and ultimately worshipped them (see 1 Kings 11). Tragically, the power of faith, which God gave to individuals to *buy truth*, is mostly used to buy into *the lie*. Esau "**sold** his own birthright for a single meal" (Heb. 12:16). The inheritance, which Esau **exchanged** for a bowl of stew, was participating as a fellow steward with the Triune-God in sacrificially carrying Their redemptive purpose for all mankind—a privileged, generational calling that both his grandfather and father *cherished* more than their own lives. The Triune-God of *Agape* "hated" (Rom. 9:13) both Esau's **self-indulgent act** as well as the worthless, **self-absorbed nature** of individualism that prompted his careless indifference to God and those who loved him.

In economic terms, to **fall** from God is to **sell** God. All the major and minor decisions of our lives come down to discerning and investing in what is of **worth** (good, quality, genuine, desirable), whether it is selecting fruits and vegetables, clothing, vehicles, houses, land, vocation and employment, friendships, a spouse, etc. In simple terms, Thomas Talbott stated the sound reason for buying into truth: "God is **good** because God is love and love is good; **love** is the one quality that makes any **life**, whether human or divine, **worth** living forever" (*The Inescapable Love of God*, p. 2).

Buying into God involves praise and worthship: an individual **appraises** God as being of greater **worth** than himself. Appraising the *worth* of "God in Christ" compared to his own worth, Paul used the phrase "surpassing value" (Phil. 3:8). He added, "I do not consider my life of any **account as dear to myself** [*emptied of self-worth-ship*], so that I may finish my course and the ministry [*stewardship*] which I received from the Lord Jesus" (Acts 20:24). Once God is *appraised* as worthy, "a treasure hidden in a field which a man found" (Matt. 13:44), one **worthships** God by sacrificial self-giving—**selling** (losing, forfeiting, debiting) **self to buy into the Nucleus of the Triune-God**. Jesus said, "Whoever wishes to save his life will lose it; but whoever **loses his life for My sake** will find it" (Matt. 16:25). To *truly* fuse into God in Christ means putting all your eggs in one basket and surrendering your plan B in the comprehensive all-in manner Abraham, Paul, and others *reciprocated* the all-true Love of God.

Lucifer's De-gene-ration Into Worthless

In order for us to exchange our *lie* for God's *truth* and enter and participate in the kingdom of the Most High, it is essential to recognize and carefully examine **the source of our fall**. Among all created beings, the archangel Lucifer was the *first* to "exchange the glory of God [*sacrificial self-giving fusion*] for the lie [*self-love, fission*];" therefore, Jesus called him "**the father of the lie**" (John 8:44). Paul referred to this *false-father* as "Belial [*lit.* **Worthless**]" (2 Cor. 6:15). *Worthless* was formerly a distinguished archangel of heaven whose name is not mentioned in the Scriptures; early theologians named him *Lucifer*—a Latin translation of "**star** [*lit. shining one or light-bearer*]" (Isa. 14:12). Jesus was a first-hand witness of Lucifer's fall, and He testified: "I was watching **Satan fall from heaven like lightning**" (Luke 10:18). Through the prophet Ezekiel, the Lord provided a detailed description of Lucifer *before* he fell:

> [12] *Thus says the Lord God, "You had the seal of perfection,* **full of wisdom** *[Agape rationale] and* **perfect in beauty** *[a self-giver].* [13] *You were in Eden, the garden of God; every precious stone was your covering [high priest of heaven]: the ruby, the topaz*

*and the diamond; the beryl, the onyx and the jasper; the lapis lazuli, the turquoise and the emerald [high priests of Israel wore a breastplate of precious stones, Ex. 28:17f]; and the gold, the workmanship of your settings [lit. tambourines] and sockets [lit. flutes], was in you. On the day that you were created they [instruments of worship] were prepared. [14] You were the **anointed cherub who covers,** and I placed you there [as a steward-leader of My worshippers]. You were **on the holy mountain of God** [dwelling with and in God Most High]; you walked in the midst of the stones of fire [heavenly beings, luminaries of God's glory] (Ezek. 28:12-14).*

This archangel was a unique creation of the Triune-God, designed with musical instruments of **worth-ship** hard-wired into his very being! He was greatly honored among created beings as an angelic high priest of heaven—a super-being of great **worth** uniquely equipped to lead all creation on an eternal journey into the fathomless **worth** of the Triune-God of *Agape*, and **invested** with authority to gather all creation into fusion in the Most High. However, Lucifer magnified, **appraised**, and esteemed *himself;* therefore, he became, instead, a mighty agent of fission named *Worthless*—a forerunner into sin (*eros*), blazing a new trail of self-discovery, self-actualization, and

self-worth-ship. Through Ezekiel, God continues to describe Lucifer's fall:

> ¹⁵You were **blameless** [eros-free] in your ways from the day you were created, until **unrighteousness** [self-love, individualism, fission] was found in you. ¹⁶By the **abundance of your trade** [exchanging the truth of God for the lie] you were **internally filled with violence** [de-gene-rate nature/DNA, predatory instinct: envy, greed, murder], and you sinned; therefore I have **cast you as profane** [unholy] **from the mountain of God** [Most High].... ¹⁷Your heart was **lifted up** because of your beauty [self-worth-ship]; you **corrupted** your wisdom by reason of your splendor [exchanged self-giving rationale for self-centered rationale]. I cast you to the ground. ¹⁸...in the unrighteousness of **your trade** [exchange] **you profaned your sanctuaries** [betrayed all the host of heaven—living stones]. Therefore I have brought fire from the midst of you; it has consumed you [implosion, fission decay], and I have turned you to **ashes** [e.g., Worthless] on the earth (Ezek. 28:15-18).

Note the economic terminology God used here: "**abundance of your trade**." The kingdom which Father, Son, and Spirit sacrificially *share* with created beings is a relational *"fullness"* (Col. 2:9-10), an "**abundant life**" (John 10:10) *gene-rated* by the sacrificial self-giving of free individuals. Peter said, "For in this way [*reciprocal gene-rosity*] **entrance** into the eternal kingdom of our Lord and Savior Jesus Christ will be **abundantly supplied** to you" (2 Pet. 1:11). Lucifer **traded** (exchanged) the superabundant fullness of *relational* self-giving Love (*Agape*) for self-love (*eros*) and became a grossly perverted creature, a treacherous *individualist* named *Worthless*. He **sold** his inheritance in the giving/receiving economy of God Most High to become a master-taker. The fact that one-third of the angels of God *followed* Worthless into darkness is evidence that he was formerly a being of great *worth* and authority: "And his tail swept away a **third** of the stars [*angels*] of heaven and threw them to the earth [*as demons*]" (Rev. 12:4). God also related the account of Lucifer's fall to the prophet Isaiah:

> *12How you have **fallen** from heaven, O **star** [lit. shining one] of the morning, O son of the dawn! [luminous being created out of the fusion of the Trinity] You have been **cut down** to the earth, you who have weakened the nations! [by deception, counterfeiting] 13But you said in your heart, **"I will** ascend to heaven; **I will raise my throne above the stars of God** [angels and children of the Most High] and **I will** sit on the mount of assembly [king of the mountain] in the*

recesses of the north [usurp God's place among His people]. ¹⁴***I will** ascend above the heights of the clouds; **I will make myself like the Most High.**" ¹⁵Nevertheless you will be **thrust down** to Sheol, to the recesses of the pit (Isa. 14:12-15).*

Lucifer was a **star** because he was a free individual willingly participating in the fusion of the Trinity by sacrificial self-giving. Lucifer's individual *worth* (beauty, wisdom, vocation, function) was inseparably connected to the *worth* of God—wholly based in the reality that he was created with the capacity to powerfully radiate the Triune-Light of the Most High. However, five times Lucifer declares "*I will....*" In self-will and self-worth-ship, this mega-star **imploded** and became a powerful, inverted vortex of fission and darkness—a **black hole**. In other words, from the time he was created, Lucifer *moved* with the life-giving vortex of the Triune-Most High in downward ascent, but then he suddenly and violently changed directions in **upward descent**.

Moses said to Israel, "To the Lord your God belong heaven and the **highest heaven** [*lit. Heb.: heaven of heavens*]" (Deut. 10:14). Paul testified that he "was caught up to the **third heaven** [*through the Son, in one Spirit, to the Father, see Eph. 2:18*] (2 Cor. 12:2), and after describing it, he added:

*⁷Because of the surpassing greatness of the **revelations,** for this reason, to keep me from **exalting myself,** there was given me a thorn in the flesh, a messenger of Satan to torment [lit. beat]—to keep me from **exalting myself!** [moving in upward descent]. ⁸Concerning this I implored the Lord [Father, Son, Spirit] three times that it might leave me. ⁹And He has said to me, "My grace [superabundant grace of Three to One Another] is sufficient for you, for power [fusion] is perfected in weakness [sacrificial self-giving; suffering Love] (2 Cor. 12:7-9).*

Evidently, angels were created in heaven, but not in *the highest heaven*; only by maturing in relational faithfulness (self-giving, self-sharing) were they lifted further into the "dwelling place," which God Most High is. These "**heavenly places**" (Eph. 1:3, 20; 2:6; 3:10; 6:12) are not physical, measurable realms but **relational fullnesses** that individuals share as the result of being fused in Oneness by all-true Love.

Long before Paul was ever introduced to *the third heaven*, the archangel Lucifer had been privy to deep places in these realms and revelations of God that effectively *tested* him. Paul's own experience and testimony of this "**third heaven...Paradise**" (2 Cor. 12:2-4) makes abundantly clear that there is something about **exposure** to these high places of extravagant gene-rosity and self-sharing that effectively **tests** the hearts of created beings: how will I use my freedom—to exalt myself or to exalt others? Jesus revealed the very heart of this test: "Is your eye **envious** because I AM *gene-rous*?" (Matt. 20:15). Will I receive and **reciprocate** God's fullness, or will I **seize** the superabundant yield and spend it on self?

The esteemed archangel Lucifer *abused* God's gift of freedom and individuality and *willfully de-gene-rated* into individualism (*eros*). As a **self-center**, Lucifer saw himself as *first*: esteeming himself *worthy* to be the object of all worship and no longer God's worshipper; and esteeming himself *worthy* to be served and above being God's servant. Once Lucifer exalted himself, he was entirely **consumed by envy of God** and rapidly imploded as a black hole. *Worthless* was cast down out of the "dwelling place" of God Most High onto the earth: "On your belly you will go, and **dust** you will eat all the days of your life" (Gen. 3:14).

Buying into his own lie, Lucifer became a **self-deceived "deceiver"** (2 John 7)—an envious impostor and usurper who has spent the subsequent ages mastering the arts of deception, counterfeiting, and seduction, to *lure* all God's creatures to follow him on this alternate, twisted path of fission: an **upward descent** of self-focus, self-discovery, and self-actualization. Selling *the lie* to each unsuspecting dupe, the false-father exploits the sum total of his victims for his own vainglory, enslaving them through addiction and fear in his counterfeit kingdom and using them as pawns in the gratification of his envy of the true God in a **cosmic custody battle**. Jesus "was led up by the Spirit into the wilderness to be tempted by the devil," and there the false-father even invited God's all-true Son to participate in this egotistical madness! Boldly quoting Scripture as a part of his customized snare, the cunning serpent offered Jesus an alluring, yet *worthless* promise— "if You fall down and worship me" (Matt. 4:1-9). God revealed both the nature and agenda of the false-father to the prophet Daniel:

> 8:4 *He did as he pleased and magnified himself [self-worth-ship].... 7:25 He will speak out against the Most* **High** *and* **wear down the saints of the Highest One....** 8:25 *And through his* **shrewdness** *[eros rationale/ calculation] he will cause* **deceit** *to succeed by his* **influence**; *and he will* **magnify himself** *in his heart, and he will* **destroy** *many while they are at ease [predator's strategy: design a counterfeit nest of rest— economic mirage–false sense of prosperity/ security]. He will even* **oppose** *the Prince of princes [Nucleus of the true kingdom], but he will be* **broken** *without human agency (Dan. 7:4, 25; 8:25).*

Coming in the form of a serpent, filled with the toxic venom of self-love and envy, this self-deceived deceiver **sold** *the lie* to Adam and Eve. God's beloved willfully **bought into** the counterfeit life of this false-father, which included his own self-centered nature, desires, rationale, and behavior. In order to **buy** into *the lie* of self-worth-ship, the man and woman had to **sell** God Most High—the very breath of the Triune-Pnuema (gene-rous seed) that first made them "a living being" (Gen. 2:7). Man's capacity to *fuse* into God and one another, spirit-into-spirit, was materially damaged; human beings became **relationally paralyzed** and treacherous—the living dead, **zombies**. Therefore, the *de-gene-rate* couple had to be *driven out* of the nest of rest of Eden where God cohabited with them and provided for them from the *gene-rous* bounty of Triune-*Agape*. The rehearsal studio, which God Most High established for them to practice and mature in the mutual-exalting dynamic of *Agape*, was closed to man and **eclipsed** into secret mystery.

This transgression and **expulsion** from the Garden is known as "the fall of man"—falling *out* of the transcendent reality of God Most High and *into* the dirt. Thereafter, mankind was con-fused to Worthless both as **partakers** of his *de-gene-rate* nature as well as **apprentices** mentored and acculturated into his own corrupt economy. The first man and woman bought into *the fallen one* and *fell*; thereafter, each and all of their subsequent offspring, including you and me, have been **held hostage in Worthless's custody** in his world of darkness and dirt.

My Empire of Dirt

In one of the final performances of his life, Johnny Cash recorded a song entitled *Hurt* on the album *American IV: The Man Comes Around* (American Recording Co., 2002). The music video shows many awards, accolades, and video clips from Cash's remarkable yet turbulent career as a celebrated lyricist and performer **esteemed** by countless fans. Curiously, Cash reflects upon his achievements, notoriety, and influence that he calls "**my empire of dirt**" and proceeds to pour a glass of red wine, representing the blood of Christ, over these commemorative symbols of his life. Interposed throughout the video of Cash are brief scenes of Jesus, thorn-crowned and crucified.

Examining the lyrics (below) reveals that Cash, in the final season of his life, had an acute need to express his agonizing regret that he was incapable of fully reciprocating and fulfilling the true love he shared with June Carter-Cash, his deceased, beloved wife. Remarkably, the lyrics were written by Trent Reznor, a member of an acid-rock band called *Nine Inch Nails*. It seems the Lord provided these lyrics as a gift to Cash from a very unlikely source simply to help him express the contents of his heart before his own death. The song is essentially Cash's **comparative appraisal** of the *worth* of Jesus' life *spent* in sacrificial Self-giving Love (downward ascent) and the *worthlessness* of his own life chasing the mirage of his career and the inability to cope with the demands of fame, which led to drug addiction and marginalizing those who loved him (upward descent).

> *I hurt myself today, to see if I still feel,*
> *I focus on the pain, the only thing that's real,*
> *The needle tears a hole, the old familiar sting,*
> *Try to kill it all away, but I remember everything,*
> *What have I become, my sweetest friend,*
> *Everyone I know, goes away in the end,*
> *And you could have it all, my empire of dirt,*
> *I will let you down, I will make you hurt,*
> *I wear this crown of thorns, upon my liars chair,*
> *Full of broken thoughts, I cannot repair,*
> *Beneath the stains of time, the feelings disappear,*
> *You are someone else, I am still right here,*
> *And you could have it all, my empire of dirt,*
> *I will let you down, I will make you hurt,*
> *If I could start again, a million miles away,*
> *I will keep myself, I would find a way.*

Cash always had a unique way of describing the realities of life in straightforward, every-day language. The raw, unembellished honesty with which he chose to appraise his own life begs this question: why are we human beings **fixated on dirt** and how did we become such a grievous **failure at relational love?** The answer lies in the fact that we *are* dirt:

The Lord God [*the "Us": Triune-Spirit/Pneuma*] **formed man** of **dust from the ground** [*dirt*], and breathed into his nostrils the **breath of life** [*spirit/*

pneuma: seed of the divine nature]; and man became a living being [*a spirit and a soul in a body*] (Gen. 2:7).

God used **dirt** as the raw resource to construct Adam's *physical* form because the "**incorruptible seed**" (1Pet. 1:23) of God's own *spiritual*, fuse-able nature of *Agape* was designed to **grow in soil** *from faith to faith*, and *from life to life*, and *from glory to glory*. The interpretation Jesus gave of His parable of the sower, the seed, and the soils helps us understand God's *in-gen-ious* plan:

But the seed in the good **soil**, these are the ones who have heard the word [*of God in Christ, reciprocal Agape*] in an honest and good heart, and hold it fast, and **bear fruit** with perseverance [*mature in Trinity-like gene-rosity as fuse-able sacrificial self-givers*] (Luke 8:15).

Adam and Eve each bought into *the lie* of the deceiver, ignorant of the fact that their body, soul, and spirit would be corrupted by *eros*. They unwittingly exchanged the *gene-rous* seed of the Triune-Creator for the *de-gene-rate* nature of the false-father and immediately became **self-conscious**: "Then the eyes of both of them were opened [*in individualism*], and they knew that they were naked…and hid themselves from the presence of the Lord" (Gen. 3:7-8). Before they fell, the man and woman were spiritually alive—conscious only of the fuse-able spirit (seed) contained *within* their frame; they were **self-unconscious**. After they fell, they became **conscious of dirt**—the *naked* earthen vessel that contained the human spirit God had breathed into them. This is how the Scriptures describe our fallen condition: "Seeing the people, Jesus felt **compassion for them**, because they were distressed and **dispirited** [*lit. Greek rhipto: cast down or thrown down; e.g., out of the Triune-Spirit; dirt-bags without a functional, fuse-able, life-giving spirit*] like sheep without a shepherd" (Matt. 9:36).

Now, this may sound humorous at first, but apart from the life-giving Pnuema of God within a human being *prevailing* over his soul (will) and body (flesh), he is nothing more than a **dispirited dirt-bag**! **Yes, our dirt-bag still contains a soul and a spirit, but our soul is tyrannized by self-will and our spirit is corrupted, inebriated, and dysfunctional—no longer fuse-able in the manner God intended. God purposed our "earthen vessel," to be filled with "glory" (2 Cor. 4:7); but instead it has been filled with Worthless's "ashes:" self-worth-ship, corruption, and fission.**

David knew this all too well, and testified, "For God Himself knows our frame [*fleshly container*]; He is mindful that we are but **dust**" (Psa. 103:4). Paul said, "If anyone thinks he is **something** [*a self-center worthy to be served*] when he is **nothing** [*a dispirited dirt-bag*] he **deceives himself** [*he has bought into Worthless's lie of individualism*]" (Gal. 6:3). The one and only hope for an inebriated, rapidly *de-gene-rating* individualist is the intervention of God in Christ who *descends* to grant him the gift of repentance.

*¹⁴The Lord God said to the serpent, "Because you have done this, **cursed** are you more than all cattle, and more than any **beast of the field** [a dirt-dweller]; on your belly you will go, and **dust you will eat** all the days of your life". ¹⁷...Then to Adam God said, "... **Cursed is the ground** [dirt] because of you; in toil you will eat of it all the days of your life. ¹⁸Both **thorns and thistles** it shall grow for you; and you will eat the plants of the field; ¹⁹By the sweat of your face you will eat bread [incarcerated in Worthless's economy—a labor-camp], till you return to **the ground,** because from it you were taken; for **you are dust, and to dust you shall return** [first death]" (Gen. 3:14-19).*

Since mankind *is* dust, and the serpent *eats* dust, our situation in the custody of the false-father is far more treacherous than we realized—we are being held captive by a "**devourer**" (Rev. 12:4). Peter warned, "Be of **sober spirit**, be on the alert. Your adversary, the devil, prowls around like a roaring lion seeking someone [*an inebriated, dispirited dirt-bag*] to **devour**" (1 Pet. 5:8). John added, "the whole world [*cursed ground and dirt-bags dwelling in it*] lies in the power of the evil one" (1 John 5:19). O, the untold agonies God suffers in this **custody battle** because *the spirit* of His beloved cannot stay clean (*eros*-free) and sober and awake!

After Adam fell, "God sent him out from the garden of Eden [*greenhouse for the growth of the seed*], to **cultivate the ground** from which he was taken" (Gen. 3:23). This is where man's participation in the economy of Worthless's world began—not "life," but *existence* in **a labor-camp** populated by "all those who are weary and heavy-laden [*lit. work to exhaustion*]" (Matt. 11:28). Alienated from the Triune-Pneuma, and outside the dynamic life of God Most High, **man became fixated on "dirt."** Heavenly, spiritual Life in *Agape* and mutual exaltation—**"the things above"** (Col. 3:1)—was lost into secret mystery. This is not because God was hiding it, but corrupt, inebriated men cannot see *the light of the knowledge of the glory of God* past the **eclipse** of their own preoccupation with earthly things and restless pursuit of self-gratification.

In *eros* rationale, *de-gene-rate* men consider the economy of the kingdom of heaven to be utter foolishness—counterproductive for *me*, yet calculating personal advantage and buying and selling one another makes perfect sense! Man's **fixation on dirt** is the cause of **turf-wars**: territorialism, disputes over land, human resources, "the love of money" (1 Tim. 3:3, 6:10; Heb. 13:5), escalating competition, hostile takeovers, and predatory war—**perpetual fission**. In the twisted likeness of the false-father, and driven and consumed *within* by our own insatiable desire, we **"sell the righteous for money** and the needy for a pair of sandals. [We] who **pant after the very dust of the earth** on the head of the helpless" (Amos 2:6-7).

See how we *de-gene-rate* dirt-bags operate:

> *23Like an **earthen vessel overlaid with silver dross** [worthless façade] are burning lips and a wicked heart. 24He who hates **disguises** it [his envious self-love] with his lips, but he lays up **deceit** in his heart [lit. inward part; eros DNA maturing]. 25When he speaks graciously **do not believe him** [do not buy "the lie"], for there are **seven abominations** in his heart [counterfeits of "the seven Spirits of God" Rev. 4:5]. 26Though his hatred **covers itself with guile** [Agape with hypocrisy] his wickedness [darkness, fission] will be revealed before the assembly [Light of individuals in fusion]. 27He who digs a pit will fall into it, and he who rolls a stone, it will come back on him. 28A **lying tongue** hates those it crushes, and a **flattering mouth** works ruin [fission decay] (Prov. 26:23-28).*

Understanding this nature and behavior gives a whole new meaning to commonly used phrases such as: *that was a low-down dirty business, dirty tricks, dirty little secrets, dirty laundry, a dirty shame, dirty cops, dirty habits, dirty jokes, filthy language, political mud-slinging, dragged through the mud,* etc. Due to the corrupt, *de-gene-rate* nature of the false-father in us, all human beings have **an affinity and magnetism to**

dirty things. Inebriated, *eros*-infected Christians are not exempt; Paul reprimanded believers saying, "There must be no **filthiness** and silly talk, or coarse jesting, which are not fitting, but rather giving of thanks [*reciprocal gene-rosity*]" (Eph. 5:4). Isaiah cried out, "Woe is me, for I am **ruined** [*de-gene-rating, decaying*]! Because I am a man of **unclean lips**, and I live among a people of **unclean lips**" (Isa. 6:5). He added: "For all of us have become like one who is **unclean** [*dispirited dirt-bags*], and **all our righteous deeds are like a filthy garment** [*eros-infected—motivated by self-interest*]; and all of us wither like a leaf [*fission decay*], and our iniquities, like the wind [*unclean spirit*], take us away" (Isa. 64:4).

Sexual immorality is also a fixation on dirt: two *dispirited* dirt-bags who are **magnetized** to that which is *"unclean"* in one another **exploiting** (buy and sell) **one another for self-gratification** (*dirty sex*) at the expense of forfeiting Father's true purpose for each of them. These acts of **con-fusion** paralyze the human spirit and open the door to the devourer who "comes only to steal, kill, and destroy" (John 10:10). Many of us believers look back with regret upon our "youthful lusts" (2 Tim. 2:22), but can we see that we were actually building an empire of dirt by sexual conquests?

James urged believers, "Putting aside all **filthiness** and all that remains of wickedness, in **humility** [*acknowledging I am a dispirited dirt-bag*] receive the **word** [*incorruptible seed*] **implanted**, which is able to save your souls [*tyrannized by self-will fixated on indulging self in the dirt*]" (James 1:21). Yes, we who have believed are *saved* (adopted), but thank God we are also "being saved [*re-gene-rated, naturalized*]" (1 Cor. 1:18). Many of us have been filled with the Spirit (Spirit-baptized), but since all of us **dirt-bags leak**, God also commands us to "be filled [*lit. be being filled*] with the Spirit" (Eph. 5:18). God spoke through Ezekiel:

> [24]*All the trees of the field [men rooted in the dirt] will know that I AM the Lord [Triune-Most High]; I **bring down** the high tree, **exalt** the low tree, **dry up** the green tree [bearing the toxic fruit of de-gene-rate DNA] and make the dry [emptied] tree **flourish** [re-gene-ration–filled with the Spirit]. I AM the Lord; I have spoken, and I will perform it (Ezek. 17:24).*

Hope for Dispirited Dirt-Bags

Thank God our great-granddaddy Adam, who *bought into* the lie and *fell* into corruption, was not the *only* "first" man! Within the **Man** Jesus—the incarnated Son of God Most High—the **seed** of the Triune-Pnuema (fuse-able DNA of *Agape*) grew in the **good soil** of His human flesh and brought forth the very fruit God intended: a prevailing, life-giving, fuse-able human spirit made adaptable and communicable to us in an "**incorruptible seed**" (1 Pet. 1:23). Paul declared, "Christ has now reconciled you **in His fleshly body** through death" (Col. 1:22). The *seed* God prepared for our *re-gene-ration* is "**Christ** [*the tested, perfected God-Man*] **in you, the hope of glory** [*participation in the Most High*]" (Col. 1:27). Paul explained:

The **first man**, Adam, became a living soul [*free individual*], the **last Adam** [*Christ Jesus*] became a **life-giving spirit** [*Man in fusion with God, spirit into Triune-Spirit*]. However, the spiritual is not first, but the natural, then the spiritual [*soil, then the eternal seed implanted*]. The first man is from the earth, **earthy** [*lit. Greek: made of dust*]; the second man is from heaven [*Son of God participating in the Most High as a Man*]. As is the **earthy**, so also are those who are **earthy** [*affinity and fixation on dirt: upward descent*]; and as is the **heavenly**, so also are those who are **heavenly** [*spiritually re-gene-rated, alive, fuse-able: downward ascent*]. Just as we have borne the image of the **earthy**, we also will bear the image of the **heavenly** [*Trinity-like: individual "life-giving spirits" in fusion*].... **Flesh and blood** [*made of dirt*] **cannot inherit the kingdom of God** [*cohabitation of "life-giving spirits" mutually exalting and indwelling one another*]; nor does the perishable [*corruptible, dispirited*] inherit the imperishable [*incorruptible, fuse-able*] (1 Cor. 15:45-50).

Each and every one of us was born into the *de-gene-rate* heredity of the false-father, Worthless,—that

earthy, eros nature that Adam willfully *bought into.*
To become "a **new** [*fuse-able*] **creation**" (2 Cor. 5:17;
Gal. 6:15), we must be "**born again** [*lit. Greek: from
above; e.g., from God Most High*]" (John 3:7), that is,
progressively *re-gene-rated* in the life-giving bloodline
of the *heavenly* God-Man Jesus. How do we do this?
Jesus is God's **choice Cornerstone**—a Man made of
dust (flesh and blood) just like you and me but in
whom "all the fullness of Deity [*Triune-Spirit*] dwells
in bodily form [*human flesh*]" (Col. 2:9). We *believe
into* God in Christ by *daily* falling upon Him:

> [44] *And he who [willingly]* **falls on this stone**
> *[perfected God-Man—Cornerstone/Nucleus
> of the Triune-God and man] will be* **broken
> to pieces** *[and re-gene-rated, reconstituted in
> fusion and filled]; but on whomever it falls,
> it will* **scatter him like dust** *[an earthy,
> dispirited dirt-bag]* (Matt. 21:44).

Abraham awakened to the transcendent reality of
God Most High as well as to the reality of his own
fallen condition. God spoke to Abraham, and Abraham
answered, "Now behold, I have ventured to speak to
the Lord, although **I am but dust and ashes**" (Gen.
18:27). Abraham knew "the father of the lie" had been
"turned to **ashes** on the earth" (Ezek. 28:18); therefore,
in humility, Abraham was essentially acknowledging
to God not only that he was a dirt-bag but also
filled with the false-father's **worthless nature** and a

willful participant in **Worthless's corrupt economy**. Abraham *appraised* the life of the *true* Triune-God far dearer than his own *worthless* life; therefore, he believed (*bought*) into Him, **exchanging** his empire of dirt for an inheritance in the "dwelling place" of the Most High. Like all mankind, Abraham had been *falling* in an upward descent, but as an emigrant to the kingdom he **changed directions** and began *moving* with the Triune-God in downward ascent.

The *promise* which Abraham received from God as an inheritance was *not* merely the *physical* land of Canaan (Palestine)—an *earthy*, preparatory rehearsal studio of literal dirt. In fact, it was *not* the **terra firma** of Palestine which Abraham considered *The Holy Land*, as many do today, but rather that **spiritual kingdom** facilitated by the mutual indwelling of *Holy, Holy, Holy* opened to mankind in the Man Jesus, "the Holy One [*Nucleus*] of God" (John 6:69):

> *⁹By faith Abraham lived as an alien in the land of promise [earthy rehearsal studio]… dwelling in tents… ¹⁰for he was looking for the **city which has foundations** [a spiritual cohabitation opened to man, built on the Cornerstone], whose **architect and builder is God** [Most High] (Heb. 11:9-10).*

The *inheritance* that Abraham received was the ability to *see forward* to the coming of **God's choice Cornerstone** and *participate in* the spiritual cohabitation of God and man built upon Him, that is, *fused* into His one body (see Eph. 1:10). Centuries after Abraham had died, the Son of the Most High came into human history on the earth as the Man Jesus, yet He testified that Abraham had *already* believed into (bought into) Him: "Abraham rejoiced to see My day [*inauguration of the cohabitation of God and man in a God-Man*] and he saw it and was glad" (John 8:56). Abraham hated his life in this world [*Worthless's empire of dirt*] (see John 12:25); therefore, he became a **kingdom emigrant** who *relocated* into God Most High by repeatedly falling upon the Cornerstone—*buying into* God in Christ by true, sacrificial self-giving. God acknowledged and greatly cherished Abraham's reciprocal self-giving and *lifted* him into Himself saying, "**Blessed be Abram of God Most High**" (Gen. 14:19). Paul explained the implications for us:

> [13]*Christ redeemed us from the curse of the Law [which condemns corrupt dirt-bags] having become a* **curse** *for us [extreme Self-forsaking Love]…* [14]*in order that* **in Christ** *[the Man perfected as a "life-giving spirit"]* **the blessing of Abraham** *[inheriting by faith and faithfulness]* **might come to the Gentiles**, *so that we would receive* **the promise of the Spirit through faith** *[the Spirit "fills" dispirited dirt-bags and re-gene-rates us in fuse-able DNA: the life-giving*

*spirit of Christ].…. ¹⁶Now the promises were spoken to Abraham and to his **seed**. God does not say, "And to seeds" as referring to many [all Abraham's offspring: Jews], but rather to **one** [the Messiah, Son of promise, born into the lineage of Isaac, David], "And to your **seed**," that is, **Christ**.…. ¹⁸God has granted the blessing to Abraham by means of a promise. ¹⁹…until the **seed** [incarnated Son] would come to whom the **promise** had been made (Gal. 3:13-19).*

Since *all* human beings are dispirited dirt-bags, the promise of the Holy Spirit could not be made to any man but *only* to the Son of God—one who would perfect in Himself, as a Man, "a life-giving spirit" and **make His own *fuse-able* human spirit communicable to us fallen creatures**. Only the life-giving human spirit of Christ is able to fuse into the Holy Spirit and through the Spirit into the Triune-God Most High. Abraham became a sharer in that promise by seeing and *buying into* the coming Son of promise, and Abraham's human spirit was awakened and raised in "the Spirit of Christ" (Rom. 8:9).

Fourteen generations after Abraham, David became a sharer in the inheritance of the kingdom that his forefather had received, entered, and cherished in Christ. Throughout his life, David also repeatedly confessed he was a dirt-bag acculturated into Worthless's economy and filled with his "ashes."

Yet, *from faith to faith*, David **awakened** to God Most High by repeatedly falling in brokenness upon the coming Cornerstone, and he was fused into the Nucleus of God in Christ as "**the man who was raised on high**" (2 Sam. 23:1). David testified:

> [7]*Who is like the Lord our God [Father, Son, Spirit in fusion by Agape], who is* **enthroned on high** *[mutually exalting One Another: downward ascent], who* **humbles Himself** *to behold the things that are in heaven and in the earth? [In the Man Jesus, God embraced and suffered the consequences of our corruption, darkness, and fission]* **He raises the poor from the dust** *[fills dirt-bags with the Spirit of His perfected Son]* **and lifts the needy from the ash heap** *[redemption from Worthless's nature and economy] (Psa. 113:7).*

The foremost purpose of the Triune-God (three Self-sharers) is to lift us *into* Themselves by transforming *dispirited* dirt-bags into "sons [*and daughters*] of the Most High" (Psa. 82:6; Luke 6:35). Abraham, David, and others such as Daniel and Paul became "**partakers of a heavenly calling**" (Heb. 3:1). These who *bought into* Christ were radically transformed from dispirited dirt-bags into true, *fuse-able* sons—reciprocal self-givers acculturated, mentored, and naturalized into the economy of heaven—and **lifted into God**

Most High. Hebrews tells us that this "great cloud of witnesses...confessed that they were strangers and exiles on the earth [*e.g., in Worthless's marketplace*]" (Heb. 12:1, 13).

Worthless's World Economy

The economy of the kingdom of the Triune-God is rooted and grounded in *Agape*—the true, **generous**, sacrificial Self-giving and Self-sharing nature of Father, Son, and Spirit. Likewise, the economic system of this world is rooted in *eros*—the corrupt, **de-gene-rate**, envious, and **self-indulgent** nature of Worthless; "the whole world [*an economic system*] lies in the power of the evil one" (1 John 5:19).

In the economy of the world, individuals debit others to credit self; in the economy of the kingdom, individuals debit self to credit others. In the world, there is no such thing as a free gift, no free lunch; in the kingdom, "**freely you received, freely give** [*reciprocal gene-rosity*]" (Matt. 10:8). Born and acculturated into this world, we automatically assume the fundamental principles, operational infrastructure, and practical function of our world economy are simply the way things are and have always been. **Eclipsed** from spiritual Reality, we are unable to see that our economic system is a direct expression of Worthless's own nature and activity. Paul explained, "the god of this world has **blinded the minds** of the unbelieving so that they might not see the light of the gospel of the glory of Christ [*invitation to participate in the economy of God Most High*]" (2 Cor. 4:4). Jesus revealed the source of these two conflicting economies:

> [9]**I AM** the door; if anyone enters through Me [*fusion into "God in Christ"*], he will be saved [*from eros individualism and famine*], and will go in and out and **find pasture** [*participate in the bountiful economy of the kingdom*]. [10]The **thief** [*false-father Worthless*] comes only to **steal, kill,** and **destroy** [*corrupt, con-fuse, allure into fission decay*]; I came that they may have **life** [*reciprocal gene-rosity, mutual indwelling in Agape*] and have it **abundantly** ["*fullness*" *of the Triune-Most High*] (John 10:9-10).

Many are surprised to discover that "Jesus, Son of the Most High" (Luke 1:32; Mark 5:7) actually entered the marketplace of Worthless's world as an **economic advisor**, saying, "I advise you to **buy** from Me gold refined by fire [*fuse-able DNA of Agape*] so that you may become **rich** [*in the economy of the kingdom*]" (Rev. 3:18). Those willing to receive and heed Jesus' counsel receive **discernment**: the ability to *distinguish between* self-giving and self-indulgence, true worth-ship and self-worth-ship, and mutual exaltation and mutual exploitation. In short, *re-gene-ration* in *Agape* enables us to "**extract the precious** [*gen-uine*] **from the worthless** [*counterfeit*]" (Jer. 15:19).

Jesus testified about Worthless, "There is no truth [*Agape, gene-rosity*] in him. Whenever he speaks a lie, he speaks out of his own nature [*eros individualism*], for he is a liar and the father of the lie" (John 8:44). This false-father is a clever impostor, a shrewd economist, and a skilled **counterfeiter**. As a former heavenly insider, Worthless (a.k.a. Lucifer) is a first-hand witness of the fusion power of God Most High and the inner workings of the economy of heaven. He uses this intimate knowledge to twist, pervert, and counterfeit all the things of God, even the Love (*Agape*) that the Triune-God is.

Paul urged, "Let your *Agape* [*sacrificial self-giving*] be without **hypocrisy** [*pretense, counterfeiting*]" (Rom. 12:9; James 3:17). *Eros* is counterfeit love or "the lie"—*Agape with* hypocrisy. Motivated by self-worth-ship, *eros* is the **pretense** of freely and sacrificially adding something of value to another at one's own **expense**, yet concealed beneath is a **calculated payoff** for personal advantage. "The sacrifice of the wicked [*pretense of costly gene-rosity*] is an abomination [*the lie*], how much more when he brings it with **evil intent!**" (Prov. 21:27). *Eros* instinctively uses pretense, deception, allurement, and counterfeiting to exploit vulnerable, relational trust for personal gain (self-gratification) and to "save" one's own life (self-preservation). Jude describes *de-gene-rate* children of the false-father as "caring for themselves; **clouds without water**...autumn trees without fruit" (Jude 12). To those whose lips are parched and crops are dying, we *appear* to be a heavy-laden raincloud accompanied by signs of thunder and lightning, yet we will not and *cannot* yield one drop!

The world we live in, both secular and religious, is **corrupted** to its core with "the lie:" mirages, counterfeits, veneers, gimmicks, false advertising, fraud, forgeries, impostors, al-lure-ments (hooks), hidden agendas, pretense and usury, predatory and parasitic cons, cornering and monopolizing markets, empire-building, oppression, inequality, slavery, and fragile, consumer-driven economies—all grounded in "earthy, natural, demonic wisdom [*eros rationale*]" (James 3:15). Perhaps John was referring to all these things when he wrote, "The Son of God [*Most High*] appeared for this purpose, **to destroy the works** [*counterfeits*] **of the devil**" (1 John 3:8). For a broader understanding, read the Lifechangers *Plumbline* entitled *Discerning the Counterfeit*.

The common denominator in all these things "from below...of this world" (John 8:23) is the **unreality of individualism** (self-worth-ship, self-will, self-indulgence) that has its origin and source in the father of the lie (*eros*). Not only do we live in Worthless's corrupt, predatory world of pretense and mutual exploitation, but we were born with this *de-gene-rate* DNA—the unreality of the lie is *in* us—and we *participate* in Worthless's marketplace by *practicing* the lie and maturing as takers in the likeness of the false-father. John warned: "Do not love the world [Worthless's economy] nor the things in the world [self-indulgence in the marketplace: crafting, selling, and buying into mirages and counterfeits]. If anyone loves the world [self in its own natural habitat: my empire of dirt], the Agape [true, gene-rous DNA] of the Father is not in him" (1 John 2:15).

The economy of the kingdom of God Most High—three life-giving Spirits in *reciprocal gene-rosity*—is transcendent, **spiritual Reality**; the more a man's spirit *awakens* and *participates* in the economy of the kingdom, the more he recognizes this physical world is entirely founded upon **spiritual unreality**. For example, in the world economy a **self-made man** is highly esteemed, yet very few recognize that it is often the nature, compulsive desires, and rationale of the false-father, Worthless, *within* that man driving him on to greatness: "I will ascend above the heights of the clouds; I will make myself like the Most High" (Isa. 14:14). However, the eternal law by which Father, Son, and Spirit Themselves live remains in effect: up is down and down is up—to *climb* is literally to *fall* in upward descent.

> *7Do not be* **deceived** *[do not buy into Worthless's economy],* **God** *[Most High]* **is not mocked***; for whatever a man sows [invests himself into], this he will also reap. 8For the one [individualist] who* **sows to** *[uses others to gratify]* **his own flesh***, will*

from the flesh reap **corruption** *[rapid fission decay], but the one who* **sows to the Spirit** *[willingly loses his life in fusion—invests himself into the economy of the Most High] will from the Spirit reap* **eternal life** *[superabundant bounty in the unshakable kingdom]" (Gal. 6:7-8).*

Now, let's look more carefully at some of the ways the Scriptures expose the source and function of the economy of this world.

Two Great Eagles

God spoke through Hosea, "My people are **bent** on turning from Me [*e.g., into corruption, self-worship—upward descent*]. Though the prophets call them to the One on **high** [*into the economy of reciprocal self-giving—mutual exaltation—downward ascent*], **none at all exalts Him**" (Hosea 11:7). *Eros* is effectively illustrated by a **hook**—an instrument *bent* on taking—*Agape* twisted and corrupted by hypocrisy. Our great-granddaddy Adam was "bent" in self-love and self-indulgence when he first *bought into* the corrupt, *de-gene-rate* nature of the deceiver in Eden and *fell* from God Most High. However, through Ezekiel, God used the imagery of two great eagles and economic inferences to describe how this **affinity for corruption** has **matured**, or *de-gene-rated*, reinforcing our **con-fusion** to Worthless:

³ Thus says the Lord God, "**A great eagle** with great wings, long pinions and a full plumage of **many colors** [God is Light—Spectrum of Three Primaries] came to Lebanon and took away the top of the cedar. ⁴He plucked off the topmost of its young twigs [people of Israel] and brought it to a **land of merchants** [Canaanites in Worthless's marketplace]; he set it in a **city of traders** [buying and selling one another]. ⁵He also took some of the seed of the land and planted it in **fertile soil** [lit. a field of seed]. He placed it beside abundant waters; he set it like a willow. ⁶Then it sprouted and became a low, spreading vine with its branches [affections] turned toward Him [true Father], but its **roots remained under it** [not yet "rooted and grounded in Agape" Eph. 3:17]. So it became a vine and yielded shoots and sent out branches. ⁷But there was **another great eagle** [an impostor] with great wings and much plumage [dark-light of individualism, no "colors"]; and behold, this vine [Israel] **bent its roots toward him** [affinity with "the father of the lie"] and sent out its branches toward him from the beds where it was planted, that he [Worthless] might water it [e.g., chasing the mirage of self-indulgence]. ⁸It was planted in good soil beside abundant waters, that it might yield branches and bear

*fruit [reciprocal gene-rosity] and become a splendid vine." [9] Thus says the Lord God, "**Will it thrive?** Will He [the "true" Triune-God] not pull up its roots and cut off its fruit, so that it **withers**—so that all its sprouting leaves wither [fission decay, famine]? And neither by great strength [self-will power] nor by many people [misplaced allegiances, counterfeit solidarity] can it be raised from its roots again. [A new Seed/Root/Man must come.] [10] Behold, though it is planted, will it thrive? Will it not **completely wither** as soon as the east wind [Vortex of "God is Jealous"] strikes it—wither on the beds [dirt] where it grew?" (Ezek. 17:3-10).*

This parable provides marvelous insight into the **custody battle** for mankind as well as the source and counterproductive nature of **Worthless's world economy**. The first eagle is the true "Most High God"; He soars in fusion power—three *eros*-free Individuals Who, in profound humility and weakness, exalt One Another by reciprocal Self-giving. The second eagle is an impostor—as an archangel who formerly participated in the fusion of his Triune-Creator. The second eagle *used* to "soar," but in his fallen state he is a **dirt-dweller** who, in pride, envy, and pretense, must now *appear* to soar. To the human eye, the only distinguishing feature is that the first eagle has "plumage of many colors," a spectrum of three

Individuals Who are One in the **Light of *Agape***; the second eagle is a solitary being who has *bought into* the **darkness of individualism**.

The cedar tree represents all mankind planted in good soil and designed to grow into the self-giving image and fuse-able likeness of the Triune-Most High as life-giving spirits. The "topmost of its young twigs" (vs. 4) represents the people of Israel whom Father, Son, and Spirit purposed to lift into Themselves by redeeming and replanting them. This account begs the question: Why did God intentionally plant Israel in "a land of **merchants**…a city of **traders**," (vs. 4) among the Canaanites who were mature, influential participants in Worthless's world economy? For that matter, why did God originally place "in the midst of the garden…the tree of the knowledge of good and evil" (Gen. 2:9)? Further, why did God permit Worthless, the deceiver, to prey upon Adam and Eve in the garden in the first place?

In order for human beings to "become partakers of the divine nature" (2 Pet. 1:4), grow in the *fuse-able* DNA of *Agape*, and participate in relational, inter-personal fusion dynamic of God Most High as *willing*, life-giving spirits, it is **necessary to test, prove, and reprove mankind** in *volitional* self-denial and *free* self-giving. In other words, in order for human beings to freely and comprehensively *buy into* "**the truth**," it is necessary for us to meet "the father of **the lie**," discern and *refuse* his counterfeit life of upward descent, and, therefore, "**overcome the evil one**" (1 John 2:13-14).

Worthless was intentionally thrown down to the earth because he inadvertently served God's purpose as the instrument by which the hearts of men are tested, proven, and re-proven in truth. Israel repeatedly failed these tests; apart from *re-gene-ration* in the tested, perfected life-giving spirit of the Man Jesus, and they were drawn as a DNA-match to the false-father: "and the people were very **unfaithful** following all the **abominations** of the nations; and they defiled the house [*cohabitation*] of the Lord which He had sanctified in Jerusalem" (2 Chron. 36:14; see 1 Kings 14:24).

These two "great eagles" operate according to **two opposite kinds of rationale**. *Eros*, known as "the lie," is a perversion and counterfeit of *Agape*—"the truth." *The lie* is a *de-gene-rate*, *eros* **nature**, but it is also a sophisticated, shrewd, and deadly form of **wisdom**.

> [13]*Who among you is wise and understanding [knowing "God is true"]? Let him show by his behavior his deeds [of gene-rosity: sacrificial self-giving] in the gentleness of* **wisdom** *[Agape rationale: jealous for one another].* [14]*But if you have* **bitter jealousy** *[jealousy of, envy] and* **selfish ambition** *[individualism: self-indulgence by self-exaltation] in your heart, do not be arrogant and so* **lie against the truth** *[Agape with hypocrisy].* [15]**This wisdom** *[eros rationale, calculation]* **is not that which comes**

down from above *[counterfeit, not from the Triune-Most High], but is **earthly** [fallen–dirt conscious], natural [dispirited], **demonic** [from the false-father, an unclean spirit].* [16]*For where **jealousy** and **selfish ambition** [eros] exist, there is disorder [confusion] and every evil thing [Worthless's marketplace].* [17]*But the **wisdom from above** [true, Triune-Most High] is first pure [holy, eros-free], then peaceable [relational], gentle [vulnerable, safe], reasonable [lit. willing to yield; self-yielding], full of mercy [forbearing, forgiving] and good fruits [gene-rosity], unwavering [unconditionally faithful], **without hypocrisy** [no calculation or hidden agenda].* [18]*And the **seed** [fuseable DNA of God in Christ] whose **fruit** is righteousness [sacrificial self-giving acts/ behavior] is **sown** in peace by those who make **peace** [gen-uine children of God intentionally practicing kingdom economics: Trinity-likeness] (James 3:13-18).*

This world functions according to an "earthy, natural, demonic wisdom," which has its **taproot** in the *bitter jealousy and selfish ambition*; the economic system of this world operates in an **eclipse** from the rationale and reality of God Most High. *Agape* and *eros* are each a form of wisdom: a rationale rooted in a nature that is manifested in behavior and yields a fruit—either life or death. Though earthy wisdom, by which *eros*-driven individualists conduct business in "the domain of darkness" (Col. 1:13), may *appear* to be highly successful, it is in fact a **counterfeit** (chasing a mirage) that is *always* counterproductive resulting in corruption, famine, and death: "there is no wisdom and no understanding and no counsel against the Lord [*true Triune-Solidarity rooted in Agape*]" (Prov. 21:30). For further understanding of God's non-negotiable wisdom, meditate on Psalm 73.

Since *de-gene-rate* human beings are inebriated, dispirited dirt-bags, they are entirely ignorant of the fact that they are being held as **captives** in the custody of a false-father whose envious purpose is to keep them **eclipsed** from their true Father. Further, since "the arrogance of your heart [*self-worth-ship*] has deceived you" (Jer. 49:16), individualists are **self-deceived deceivers** who imagine themselves to be free, original thinkers whose selfish ambitions are *their own* inspiration! They are blind to the fact that the earthy, dirt-conscious wisdom of this false-father (the original individualist) wields its powerful influence over their practical, day-to-day lives and decisions: "through his shrewdness, he will cause deceit to succeed by his **influence**" (Dan. 8:25). See how Jesus distinguished these two kinds of wisdom:

> [21] **Jesus** *[the Son] rejoiced greatly in the* **Holy Spirit***, and said, "I praise You O* **Father***, Lord of heaven and earth, that You have*

*hidden these things [kingdom economics] from the **wise** and **intelligent** [dispirited dirt-bags mature in eros rationale and skilled in Worthless economy] and have revealed them to **infants** [newborns re-gene-rating in Agape–the true, fuse-able DNA of God Most High]. Yes, Father, for this way was well-pleasing in Your sight"* (Luke. 10:21).

Isaiah foretold the coming of the Son Jesus: "The people who were **sitting in darkness** [*eros individualism*] **saw a great Light** [*Triune-God in Christ*], and those who were **sitting in the land and shadow of death** [*Worthless's marketplace*], upon them **a Light dawned**" (Isa. 9:2; Matt. 4:16). Jesus had a unique perspective on those who *invest themselves* into the economy of Worthless's world:

*[16]But to what shall I compare the men of this generation [eros de-gene-rates] and what are they like? They are like **children** [immature, self-indulgent, self-willed orphans] **who sit** [idle, fruitless] **in the marketplace** [a place to buy and sell one another], and **call to one another** [i.e. on cell phones–a pocket-sized idol–used to arrange eros payoffs] [17]and say, "We **played the flute for you** [Agape with hypocrisy], and **you did not dance** [i.e. to our tune–do and say what we want–manipulation, control]; **we sang***

a dirge [sad song; seeking attention as a self-center by extracting pity and sympathy; seeking one who understands and accepts me] and **you did not weep** [crab-bucket–pulling you down into their fruitless darkness; diverting your attention from God; stealing your fruit-bearing potential]. [18]For John the Baptist has come eating no bread and drinking no wine [self-emptying in preparation for "the fullness" in Christ] and you say, "He has a demon!" [19]The **Son of Man** [Jesus] has come eating and drinking and you say "Behold, a gluttonous man and a drunkard, a friend of tax collectors and sinners!" [Is it possible to please children of "the lie" except by participating in their con-fusion, making them your object and focus, and doing it their way?]. **Yet wisdom** ["from above"–Trinity-like "Way" of free, reciprocal Agape considered foolishness by the world] **is vindicated** [proven "true"] **by all her children** [takers re-gene-rated into sacrificial self-sharers: fruitful steward-heirs of the kingdom] (Matt. 11:16-19).

Over the years, my Dad has passed on to me as an inheritance many gifts of true wisdom, but among the most memorable and valuable is this: **You don't have to put a lid on a crab bucket**. As soon as one crab begins nearing the rim, the others, motivated by the same instinct of self-preservation, pull him down, and climb on him attempting to secure their own escape. The envious false-father, the author and agent of **relational fission**, has a relatively easy job because we eros-infected individualists do his work *for* him; we unwittingly accomplish his purpose: "**I will raise my throne above the stars** [*children*] **of God**" (Isa. 14:13).

We fleshly, self-focused Christians are among Worthless's most effective helpers who gratify, preserve, and promote ourselves by biting, devouring, and **consuming one another** (Gal. 5:15). In order to feel better about myself, I pull others down by fault-finding and calculated criticism. Unconsciously, I have *bought into* **Worthless's lie: by standing on others I can make myself higher**. When I put human beings "beneath my feet" as I would an enemy, the *actual* enemy is exalted; I am manifesting the false-father's nature of **self-exaltation**! This dynamic of relational fission is very powerful, keeping all of us injured, suspicious, alienated, and abased in the dirt—**plummeting in upward descent**—while the father of the lie simply reclines and watches us gratify his envious desire! Paul identified **the crab bucket:**

> [15] Where then is that sense of blessing [reciprocal gene-rosity] you had? For I bear you witness that, if possible, you would have plucked out your eyes and given them to me [extreme self-forsaking Love; jealous-for Love]. [16] So have I

become your enemy by telling you the truth?
[17] They [sons of Worthless] **eagerly seek you,**
not commendably, but they wish to **shut you**
out *[of God Most High; prevent true fusion]*
so that you will **seek them** *[con-fusion:*
urging your participation in Worthless's
marketplace to exact an eros payoff from you;
i.e. play poker with us, ante up!]. [18] But it is
good to always be **eagerly sought out** *in a*
commendable manner [to participate with
one another in the kingdom economy]....
[19] My children, with whom I am **in labor**
[true suffering love] until Christ [the gene-
rous Seed] is formed in you (Gal. 4:15-19).

Do not underestimate the power of the world to
magnetize and **captivate**—a grand mirage, which
Worthless devised and established as an expression of
his own nature and dedicated to himself. Concealed
beneath the façade of a bountiful marketplace, full
of alluring counterfeits lies a mighty, **inverted vortex**
(black hole) designed to dissuade and prevent us from
emigrating into God Most High and to systematically
destroy us by fission decay. The false-father "**does not**
allow his prisoners to go home" (Isa. 14:17; see also
Matt. 12:29).

It is hard to **enter** the kingdom of God (Acts
14:22; Matt. 19:23-24). Yet, since God does not use
coercion, but only grants *freedom*, it is very easy to
exit the kingdom (Gal. 1:6). Like a gambling addict

convinced he is finally at the lucky blackjack table, with nearly effortless ease he can plunge deeper *into* the world (Matt. 7:13-14); but, apart from a **Redeemer**, it is absolutely impossible to get himself *out*. In other words: it costs everything to **buy into** the kingdom (Matt. 13:44), but it is so easy to **exchange** it; and, it is so **convenient** and exciting to *buy into* the world, but how **excruciating** it is to *sell* it (see Gal. 6:14).

Desiring Desire

The economy of this world has a **subterranean**, **toxic taproot**: "bitter jealousy [*envy*] and selfish ambition" (James 3:14). This taproot is the *nature* of Worthless, the father of the lie. This taproot is **concealed beneath the dirt** *within* us. Jesus said, "You are of your father the devil, and you want to do the **desires** of your father" (John 8:44). The *eros* nature of the false-father manifests itself in and through us as "greedy desires" [*literal Heb.: **desiring desire***] (Num. 11:4).

Beneath our fixation on specific vices, material things, and ambitions is "**desiring desire**" itself *for* **self**—a desire that is never satisfied no matter what variety or quantity of things, opportunities, or achievements you feed it. Paul called this "being corrupted in accordance with the **lusts of deceit** [*insatiable desire*]" (Eph. 4:22). Self-counsel is a false witness: the lie *within* me assures me that my desires *can* be satisfied, when, in fact, they *cannot*. The insatiable addiction of *desiring desire* may be compared to a parched man who chugs seawater to quench his thirst. "Sheol and Abaddon are **never satisfied**, nor are the eyes of man ever satisfied" (Prov. 27:20). Habakkuk added,

> [4]*Behold, as for the* **proud one** *[individualist], his* **soul** *is not right within him [tyrannized by self-will, self-worth-ship]; but the righteous will live by his faith [or faithfulness; e.g.,, reciprocal gene-rosity with God].* [5]*Furthermore, wine betrays the* **haughty man**, *so that he does not stay at home [restless self-indulgence]. He* **enlarges his appetite** *like Sheol [a black hole], and he is like death,* **never satisfied** *[desiring desire itself for self]. He also gathers to himself all nations and* **collects to himself all peoples** *[exploiting human resources to build an empire of dirt] (Hab. 2:4-5).*

Describing *eros* as a restless appetite, Bob Mumford observed that a **shark** can never stop swimming. This predator is an **opportunist** that smells blood from great distances, calculates vulnerability and distress, and gratifies itself at the expense of others. However, a shark *must* keep swimming—perpetually seeking something to devour—otherwise it will drown; this creature is literally **a slave of its own appetite**. Worthless is a predatory opportunist enslaved to his own appetite: "When the devil had finished every temptation, he left Jesus until an **opportune** time" (Luke 14:13).

Not only is the false-father *himself* an opportunist but his *de-gene-rate nature* is within us. Paul testified, "For **sin** [*e.g., my eros nature*], taking an **opportunity** through the commandment [*the Law*], **deceived me** [*e.g., I bought into the lie and mirage of self-righteousness*] and through it **killed me** [*the living dead: alive to self, dead to others*]" (Rom. 7:11). In the likeness of the false-father, Judas matured as an opportunist: "The chief priests…promised to give him money. And Judas began seeking how to betray Jesus at an **opportune** time" (Mark 14:11). Opportunists are "**slaves**, not of our Lord Jesus Christ but **of their own appetites** [*desiring desire*]; and by their smooth and flattering speech [*pretense, allurement*] they deceive the hearts of the unsuspecting" (Rom. 16:18).

The marketplace of Worthless's world is a **consumer-driven** economy. **Capitalism** can only capitalize on consumerism. The common denominator among all human beings is *desiring desire*; **opportunists** exploit the vulnerability and predictability of the compulsive self-indulgence of the masses. **Socialism** (communism) initially thrives by its own hypocrisy. Reacting to the gross, unrestrained indulgence of the previous king, regime, or administration, socialist revolutionaries promise **equality** to all; however, they are entirely unprepared for the **absolute corruption** that accompanies absolute power. Those who hold the reins in the socialist committee are consumed by envy and selfish ambition—they jockey for power and become ruthless **opportunists** who oppress and exploit their citizens by making them *property of the state* and **capitalize on them as a collective labor force**.

Both capitalism and socialism are constructs of corruptible man, fashioned in the *de-gene-rate* image of the first predatory opportunist and hypocrite, Worthless. In both of these systems, individuals are expendable. Both of these economic systems are variations of Frankenstein's monster that rages out of control and systematically tyrannizes and destroys all who are in its path, including its creators.

Consider all the various kinds of **free enterprisers** restlessly seeking a name for themselves and a place of their own in this world. In order to maintain a competitive edge over one another in the crab bucket, they must constantly sniff out business opportunities or devise fraudulent ones. Though they are free to do this, in reality, are they not **enslaved in Worthless's marketplace** and plummeting in upward descent? Consider all the entrepreneurial endeavors that constitute the essential infrastructure of the world economy; how much of this activity is motivated by the envy and selfish ambition of the false-father manifested through his unwitting captives? For instance, a "**hedge fund**" is a limited partnership of investors (in con-fusion) that uses high risk methods, such as investing with borrowed money, in hopes of realizing large capital gains.

Paul sought to awaken us half-inebriated believers to the reality of opportunism: "Do not give the devil an opportunity" (Eph. 4:27). "For you were called to freedom, brethren; only do not turn your freedom into an **opportunity** for the flesh [*self-indulgence, self-will, self-worth-ship*], but through *Agape* [*sacrificial self-giving Love*] **serve one another** [*participate in the economy of the Most High*]" (Gal. 5:13).

Desiring desire is both the *cause* of envy and selfish ambition and its compounded *effect*. Each repeated attempt to gratify insatiable desire invariably precipitates a deeper sense of **emptiness**, regardless of whether a man considers his attempt to be successful or not. This emptiness, in turn, leads to **desperate discontent** and further predatory and parasitic schemes. Bob Mumford called this the law of diminishing returns. **Opportunists must rapidly adapt and mature to survive this *free-fall* into famine**. Jesus observed, "The sons of this age are more **shrewd** in relation to their own kind [*predators outwitting inferior predators*] than the sons of light [*not yet mature in reciprocal gene-rosity*]" (Luke 16:8).

In the economy of the kingdom, however, self-emptying and reciprocal self-giving result in **fullness**. Only two basic forms of desire exist: *desiring desire* itself *for* self (*eros* individualism) *or* the desire of the Trinity *for* One Another and *for* us (*Agape*) "made full" in us and manifested through us *for* God and one another. "He who separates himself [*fission*] seeks **his**

own desire" (Prov. 18:1), but "***Agape*...does not seek its own** [*desire*]" (1 Cor. 13:5).

Consider emptiness and fullness in dimensional terms. The self-referential dynamic of *desiring desire*—loving and indulging oneself to death—leads to **implosion**: a shrinking, **one-dimensional** existence, a prison cell of individualism that keeps getting smaller especially as a man's empire of dirt gets bigger. As an individual participating in the fusion of the Trinity, Lucifer was formerly a full-bodied "star" (Isa. 14:12), **filled** with the glory of God. Yet, envy and selfish ambition (*desiring desire*) caused him to **implode** into a dimensionless (one-dimensional) point—an inverted vortex, a black hole. This **empty** individualist named Worthless now vacuums into his own fission decay all those who come into proximity of his influence by *buying* his lie, and he reduces them to ashes. The *de-gene-rate*, self-conscious nature of this deceiving serpent within a human being *first* compels a man to eat his own tail and *consume himself*, *then*, in **one-dimensional emptiness**, he instinctively *preys upon others* in a restless attempt to gratify (fill) his insatiable desire.

Conversely, as the Triune-God *re-gene-rates* a taker and opportunist into "a life-giving spirit"—an individual capable of denying, emptying, and sacrificially giving himself—this fuse-able man participates in the economy of the kingdom, which is a **four-dimensional Reality**. Within the Nucleus of Jesus Christ—the combined and combining God-Man—Father, Son, Spirit, and individual human beings all participate and share in "**the fullness**" of reciprocal gene-rosity:

> [17]...that Christ [the God-Man Nucleus may dwell in your hearts through faith; and that you, being rooted and grounded in Agape [sacrificial self-giving Love], [18]may be able to comprehend with all the saints [an us in Trinity-like oneness] what is the **breadth** and **length** and **height** and **depth** [four-dimensional cohabitation/economy], [19]and to know the Agape of God that surpasses knowledge, that you may be **filled** up to all **the fullness of God** (Eph. 3:17-19).

Now, I realize that attributing the design and function of the world economy to the fallen archangel Worthless is the granddaddy of all conspiracy theories, yet the Scriptures clearly and consistently affirm this: "We know that we are of God, and that the whole world lies in the power of the evil one" (1 John 5:19; see 2 Cor. 4:4). The Scriptures testify that "the father of the lie" is a mighty, unclean spirit who operates from concealment and exerts tremendous influence over "**this present evil age**" (Gal. 1:4). If you have the courage, let's press on to discover what the Scriptures are trying to tell us about *desiring desire* and its impact on the economy of this world!

In 1886, the Russian author Leo Tolstoy wrote a short story entitled, "How Much Land Does a Man Need?" that powerfully illustrates man's fixation on dirt and an insatiable pursuit of an empire of dirt. In 1996, The Trinity Forum published Tolstoy's story along with a very valuable foreword by Os Guinness on the nature of world economics; below is an excerpt:

> *As we seek money and possessions, the pursuit grows into a **never-satisfied desire that fuels avarice** [greed, coveting]—described by the Bible as a vain "chasing after wind," by Buddhists as "craving," and by moderns as "addiction." The very Hebrew word for **money** (kesef) comes from a verb meaning "**to desire**" or "languish" after something [desiring desire]....The insatiability touches two areas—getting what we do not have and clutching on to what we do [eros: acquire, possess, control]....**Insatiability** is commonly linked to **being consumed** [black hole]. Individuals and societies that devote themselves to money soon become devoured by it. Or as the Bible reiterates, we become what we **worship** [worth-ship]. Money almost literally seems to eat people away, drying up the sap of their vitality and withering their spontaneity, generosity, and joy [fission decay].... "**Nothing gained** [emptiness, futility: upward descent]" is the*

final lesson of insatiability (Os Guinness, Foreword to Tolstoy's How Much Land Does a Man Need?, The Trinity Forum, p. 5-7).

The Old Testament makes a direct connection between monetary currency and *desiring desire*, and the New Testament calls it "the **wealth** [*lit. mammon*] **of unrighteousness**" (Luke 16:9, 11; 2 Pet. 2:12-22). The Greek term *mammon* goes beyond defining money as an inanimate object; it actually *personifies* money as a god that is served and worth-shipped in place of the true God—a god **exchanged** for God.

All my life I have believed money to be intrinsically neutral and that the motive of the user alone determined whether it was good or evil. I considered money to be in the same category as firearms—essentially neutral instruments: used to hunt for food for your family and protect them from violent intruders; or used to commit armed robbery or murder. However, recognizing that the Scriptures do not describe money as intrinsically or morally neutral has led me to examine the **origin and source of money** and its' inherently addictive nature.

The currency of the eternal kingdom is sacrificial self-giving and self-sharing; therefore, **God did not design or create money**. In Eden, Adam and Eve did not need cash or credit cards! Monetary currency (*to desire, mammon*) is a construct and essential element of Worthless's corrupt economy devised and developed *after* the fall as a substitute or **counterfeit** for self-giving and self-sharing. Mentored by the false-father, and in collaboration with him, corrupt human beings developed monetary currency to serve as the **medium of exchange** in the economy of the world—the **essential lifeblood** that keeps Worthless's marketplace flowing. In a corrupt economic system where participants repeatedly buy and sell one another to gratify their insatiable desire, money is an invention of necessity, convenience, and control.

In the corrupt rationale of this fallen world, monetary currency seems so practical and beneficial, yet the power of *desiring desire* is inherent in the origin, existence, and use of money. Money was shrewdly designed to resonate with and correspond to our *eros* nature and to be the indispensable means by which man may acquire, possess, and control dirt: land, material things, and human beings. As a perversion and counterfeit for sacrificial self-giving, **money keeps mankind fixated on dirt**, abased and enslaved in Worthless's marketplace, and eclipsed from God Most High. Each time the Lord prompts us to sacrificially give money, and especially when He invites us to enrich an undeserving enemy with precious seed money (Matt. 5:38f), we face the intrinsic power of "mammon" and its *hold* on us.

The only way to discern between a *gen-uine* thing, person, spirit, or idea and its *counterfeit* is to determine its origin and source.

*21 The Pharisees questioned Jesus, saying, "Teacher, we know that You speak and teach correctly, and You are not partial to any, but teach the way of God in truth. 22 Is it lawful for us to pay taxes to Caesar, or not?" 23 But He detected their **trickery** [opportunism: Agape with hypocrisy] and said to them, 24 "**Show Me a denarius** [Roman coin valued at one day's wage for a blue-collar worker]. **Whose likeness and inscription does it have** [e.g., what is its source]?" They said, "**Caesar's**." 25 And He said to them, 'Then render to Caesar the things that are **Caesar's** [wealth of unrighteousness in Worthless's economy] and to God the things that are **God's** [sacrificial self-giving in the economy of the Most High]" (Luke 20:21-25).*

To discern the origin and source of money, do not *look at* it, but *see through* it, as Jesus did. Recognizing that "**mammon**" is a counterfeit construct of Worthless's world economy designed to *inflame* insatiable desire and that is a conduit of his spiritual influence, affects the way we *re-gene-rating* children of God see money, relate to money, and use money. In the world economy, we love money and *use* people to get money; in the economy of the kingdom here on earth, we love people and *use* money to value and *cherish* people. John described it this way, "But whoever has the **world's goods** [*mediums of exchange in Worthless's marketplace*] and sees his brother in need and closes his heart against him [*unwilling to give/share*], how does **the *Agape* of God** [*gene-rous DNA*] abide in him?" (1 John 3:17). Jesus advised:

> *⁹And I say to you, make **friends** [true treasure] for yourselves by means of the **wealth** [lit. mammon] **of unrighteousness** [e.g., overcome the inherent power of mammon by using it to sacrificially enrich one another in reciprocal gene-rosity], so that **when it fails** [historically, world currencies and economies inevitably and repeatedly implode, resulting in famine], they will receive you into the **eternal dwellings** [the spiritual, relational kingdom]. ¹⁰He who is **faithful** in a very little thing is faithful also in much [incorruptible DNA and behavior]; and he who is **unrighteous** [corrupt] in a very little thing is unrighteous [self-indulgent] also in much. ¹¹Therefore, if you have not been **faithful in the use of unrighteous wealth** [sacrificially and gene-rously investing money into others], who will **entrust the true riches** [relational, inter-personal "fullness"] to you?* (Luke 16:9-11).

In other words, Jesus, our economic Advisor, gave counsel to **overcome and conquer the**

inherent power of mammon (Worthless's medium of exchange) by using our money to **enrich others** in the way we are tempted to hoard it and use it to **enrich ourselves**. Following Jesus' advice means that I, the individualist, must **sell my share** in Worthless's economy and use it to **buy shares** in the economy of the unshakable kingdom. Only by making this *exchange* will I discover that true treasure is reciprocal gene-rosity with true friends: "Greater love has no one than this, that one **lay down his life** for his **friends** [*e.g., downward ascent*]" (John 15:13).

The two great eagles and the two kinds of wisdom we previously studied are also described as **two foundations** (Matt. 7:24-27)**: "the sand"** of *eros* individualism, self-worth-ship, mutual usury, and fission; and "**the rock**" of *Agape*—reciprocal gene-rosity, fusion, and relational, inter-personal **solidarity**. As Jesus predicted and history confirms, the interconnected economies of the world and the money (mammon) are destined to repeatedly "**fail**" because they are **built on the sand**, that is, upon opportunists in *con-fusion* who lack the **cohesive ingredient** of sacrificial self-giving DNA. The economies and financial institutions in Worthless's world are *not* storm worthy, therefore, looking to a financial portfolio for a sense of security is the investment of "a foolish man who built his house on the sand," rather than upon "the rock" of true Triune-Solidarity.

The God-Man Jesus *knew* "the kingdom of heaven" and He *knew* "the world" from **first-hand experience**; therefore, He *advised* us how to discern and accurately *appraise* Worthless's world economy and relocate our investment into the economy of God Most High:

> *19* ***Do not store up*** *for yourselves* ***treasures on earth*** *[in Worthless's corrupt economy], where moth and rust destroy, and where* ***thieves*** *[opportunists] break in and steal [fission decay in all creation]. 20 But store up for yourselves* ***treasures in heaven*** *[economy of the incorruptible kingdom], where neither moth nor rust destroys, and where thieves do not break in or steal; 21 for where your* ***treasure*** *is, there will your heart [affections, desire] be also. 22 The eye is the lamp of the body; so then if your* ***eye is clear*** *[eros-free] your whole body will be full of* ***light*** *[relational, inter-personal fusion by Agape; treasuring and enriching others]. 23 But if your* ***eye is bad*** *[self-focused] your whole body will be full of* ***darkness*** *[individualism: desiring desire, predatory opportunism, self-indulgence]. If then the light that is in you is darkness [Agape with hypocrisy], how great is* ***the darkness*** *[a black hole]! 24 No one can serve two masters [an individual cannot be in two nuclei at once]; for either he will* ***hate*** *the one [God in Christ] and* ***love*** *the other*

*[self-worth-ship], or he will be **devoted** to one [perpetually lose his life into God in Christ] and **despise** the other [hate his own autonomous life in this world]. **You cannot serve God and wealth** [lit. mammon; two incompatible economies] (Matt. 6:19-24).*

The fact that Jesus clearly defined **money** as a medium of **idolatry** raises this question: Is it possible to function *in* this world economy and not be *of* this world economy? More precisely, is it possible for a "son [*or daughter*] of the Most High" (Luke 6:35) to operate a business in this world that lies in the power of the false-father yet **steward** that business according to the economic principles of the kingdom that please our true Father? Jesus provided an answer, "Father…I do not ask You to take them **out of the world**, but to keep them from the evil one" (John 17:15). As sons and daughters of the Most High, we are called to **overcome, conquer, and master mammon**, and as overcomers, we are commissioned to follow Jesus in **carrying the Light of the economy of the kingdom**, within ourselves, directly into the midst of Worthless's marketplace!

Our challenge is to steward and use "the wealth [*mammon*] of unrighteousness" *for* the purposes of righteousness, ever conscious of its inherent power to seduce, corrupt, and captivate. According to Paul, we are called to be "children of God [*Most High*] above reproach [*eros-free givers*] **in the midst of a crooked**

and perverse generation [*corrupt takers, opportunists*], among whom you appear as **lights** [*lit. stars; fusion luminaries*] in the world" (Phil. 2:15). It seems J.R.R. Tolkien had this real-life challenge in mind when he penned *The Lord of the Rings*, in which the main character, Frodo, is commissioned to carry the ring of power that is intrinsically evil.

Perhaps there is no more effective way to be a luminary in "the domain of darkness" than as **a godly** (Trinity-like) **business person**—a *gene-rous* ambassador of the kingdom *within* Worthless's marketplace. Meet some forerunners: "Now Abram was **very rich** in livestock, in silver and in gold" (Gen. 13:2). Abram had no desire to accumulate wealth or build an empire of dirt for himself; rather, as an **incorruptible steward** of God's promised inheritance, he repeatedly forfeited his interests in this world and kept "**seeking the things above**" (Col. 3:1). Therefore, Abram was **free** to be very rich *and* to be "Abram of God Most High" (Gen. 14:19). In addition to the true, spiritual wealth of reciprocal gene-rosity with Abram, God delighted in adding material things to him since he had set his whole desire upon God and the tail of his material wealth never wagged the dog. Joseph and Daniel were also men who had vast resources at their disposal yet remained *all-true* in the economy of the kingdom as **steward-sons of the Most High**.

These men willingly shared God's economy of values and worth, recognizing that "**true riches**" (Luke 16:11) **are *not* material**. Some may argue here that God directed Moses to construct the ark of the covenant of **pure gold** and instructed Solomon to overlay the entire temple in gold. However, we must appraise these things spiritually. The way God (a Triune-Spirit) introduces natural-minded, earth-bound human beings to *spiritual* reality is first to illustrate it in the *natural* (1 Cor. 15:46). God purposed the tabernacle and the temple to serve merely as **rehearsal studios** full of props where Israel could practice reciprocal gene-rosity and awaken spiritually. The true riches, inheritance, and dwelling God desires is literally human beings, "living stones" *re-gene-rated* as life-giving spirits and fused into the God-Man Jesus. See how the Triune-God actually **appraised** those physical rehearsal studios:

> [6]*But if you or your sons indeed* turn away from following Me [fission, upward descent], and do not keep My commandments and My statutes [kingdom economics] which I have set before you, and go and serve other gods and worship them [con-fusion], then I will cut off Israel from the land which I have given them, and **the house** which I have consecrated for My name, **I will cast out of My sight....** [8]**And this house** [full of gold] **will become a heap of ruins** [worthless]; everyone who passes by will be astonished and hiss and say, "Why has the Lord done thus to this land and to this house?" [9]And

*they will say, "Because they **forsook the Lord
their God** [exchanged glory for corruption],
**who brought their fathers out of the
land of Egypt**, and adopted [bought into]
other gods and worshiped them and served
them, therefore the Lord has brought all this
adversity on them"* (1 Kings 9:6-9).

Though money *appears* to be an inanimate,
material object, it is actually a **living** thing because it
is *animated* by the activity of an unclean spirit, "the
god of this world" (2 Cor. 4:4). Money (mammon) is
one of the primary conduits of Worthless's dynamic
influence and control over dispirited dirt-bags. The
de-gene-rate, *eros* nature (desiring desire), which I have
in common with the false-father, causes money (his
chosen conduit/idol/god) to be alive to me and me to
it. It is my *desire* for money and my *faith* in money—
buying into mammon—that makes it a living
relationship of con-fusion. When money is exposed
as essentially *worthless*—**a camouflaged medium of
Worthless's control**—then I no longer *desire* it, and
money becomes **dead** to me. He who has overcome
and mastered mammon is *free* to be **alive** to the
Triune-God as a faithful, incorruptible steward of the
kingdom. To this *gene-rous* one, God can *freely* entrust
material wealth; and through this *gene-rous* one, God
can freely and miraculously and bountifully provide
for the spiritual and physical needs of His people.

Though some believers have overcome mammon, for multitudes of others the pursuit or possession of material wealth has been the cause of their **abasement in the dirt** (upward descent) and the forfeiture of their spiritual inheritance of participating in God Most High. Paul warned, "For the love of money is a **root** of all sorts of evil [*Worthless's taproot*], and some by longing for it [*desiring desire*] have **wandered away from the faith** [*fission, con-fusion*] and **pierced** themselves with many griefs" (1 Tim. 6:10). If the power of mammon within the secular marketplace is not complicated enough, this hypocrisy is exponentially compounded when God's people, who are called to be sacrificial self-givers, participate in Worthless's economy as *eros*-driven takers. **Religious opportunists** shrewdly bait the *eros* hook within themselves with the true and living things of God in order to effectively snare and exploit God's people! Jesus encountered these men:

> [25] *Woe to you scribes and Pharisees,* **hypocrites!** *[pretenders, impostors] …* **inside** *[de-gene-rate nature, DNA] they are full of* **robbery** *and* **self-indulgence** *[desiring desire].* [27] *…* **inside** *they are full of dead men's bones [opportunists, devourers] and all uncleanness [corruption].* [28] *…* **Inwardly** *you are full of hypocrisy and lawlessness [the lie]….* [33] *You serpents, you* **brood of vipers** *[predatory sons of the false-father], how will you escape the sentence of hell? (Matt. 23:25-33).*

Paul testified, "I was formerly a blasphemer and a persecutor and a **violent aggressor**" (1 Tim. 1:13). Before Paul was *re-gene-rated* into a *fuse-able* man, he was **Saul the Pharisee**—a self-righteous opportunist whose insatiable desire was to **promote himself** up the ranks of his religious sect by devouring those whom the Pharisees envied and hated: followers of Christ.

> *8:3Saul began **ravaging** the church, entering house after house, and **dragging off** men and women, he would put them in prison. 9:1Now Saul, still **breathing threats and murder** [unclean spirit of Worthless] against the disciples of the Lord, **went** [as an opportunist] **to the high priest and asked for letters from him** to the synagogues at Damascus, so that if he found any belonging to **the Way** [e.g., practicing kingdom economics], both men and women, he might **bring them bound to Jerusalem** [e.g., to sell in Worthless's religious marketplace for his own advancement] (Acts 8:3; 9:1).*

This religious variety of the *de-gene-rate*, predatory nature manifested in Saul and the Pharisees did not originate with them; it had been passed down through the generations of Israel from ancient times. God filled the prophet Ezekiel with His "lamentation for the **princes of Israel**." These wayward sons whom God loved were **bent** toward the false-father, partakers of his corrupt nature, maturing in his insatiable desire, and mentored by Worthless as opportunists trained to prey upon their own countrymen:

> *²What was your mother [Israel]?* **A lioness among lions!** *She lay down among young lions [prostituted herself to corrupt nations], she* **reared her cubs.** *³When she brought up [mentored] one of her cubs, he became a lion, and* **he learned to tear his prey; he devoured men**" *(Ezek. 19:2-3).*

The law of Moses was designed by God as a preliminary training and "tutor" (Gal. 3:24) to introduce His earth-bound, slave-minded people to the spiritual kingdom and allow them to practice participating in the economy of reciprocal gene-rosity. However, Israel **corrupted** all these practicums by bringing in a **syncretism** (mixture) of Worthless's economy:

> *⁴Hear this, you who trample the needy, to do away with the humble of the land, ⁵saying, "When will the new moon be over, so that we may* **sell** *grain, and the Sabbath, that we may open the wheat* **market**, *to make the bushel smaller and the shekel bigger, and to* **cheat with dishonest scales** *[lit. balances of deception], ⁶so as to* **buy the helpless for money** *and the needy for a pair of sandals,*

*and that we may **sell the refuse** [worthless portion] of the wheat?" (Amos 8:4-6).*

Paul made clear that it is not only religious Jews who exploit their sacred faith in futile attempts to gratify their insatiable desire; believers in Christ who remain tyrannized by *eros* and acculturated in Worthless's economy do the very same. Paul testified, "For we are not like many, **peddling** the word of God [*religious opportunists*], but as from sincerity, but as from God [*true Triune-Love*], we speak in Christ in the sight of God" (2 Cor. 2:17). Paul added:

> *15Some, to be sure, are **preaching Christ even from envy and strife** [self-exaltation, competition, fission], but some also from good will [a willing, life-giving spirit]; 16the latter do it out of **Agape** [sacrificial self-giving], 17the former proclaim Christ out of **selfish ambition** [self-promotion, opportunism] rather than from pure [eros-free] motives, thinking to cause me distress in my imprisonment [pulling me down to lift themselves higher] (Phil. 1:15-17).*

While restlessly cruising like sharks in the world, opportunists sometimes encounter the real things of God. They instinctively recognize and appraise these real things as an opportunity and seek to twist and corrupt them to gratify their own insatiable desire.

Simon the magician believed in Jesus because of the words and works of the Spirit through the apostles, yet as a dispirited dirt-bag, he was deeply acculturated in Worthless's marketplace, and old habits die hard!

> [18]Now when Simon saw that the Spirit was bestowed through the laying on of the apostles hands, he offered them money, [19]saying, "Give this authority to me as well, so that everyone on whom I lay my hands may receive the Spirit as well [religious opportunism]."[20]But Peter said to him, "May your silver perish with you, because you thought you could **obtain the gift of God with money.** [21]You have no portion [shared inheritance] in this matter, for your heart is not right before God…. [23]For I see that you are in the **gall of bitterness** [motivated by Worthless's envy and selfish ambition] and in the **bondage of iniquity** [enslaved in self-indulgence and self-worth-ship]" (Acts 8:18-23).

Economics and Worth-ship

In order for us, as immature believers, to *grow* in Trinity-like *Agape*, it is important to recognize that we have not yet become *acculturated* into the **economy of values**, or worth, of our Triune-God. We have not yet learned how to "**extract the precious from the worthless**" (Jer. 15:19). Can we acknowledge that we are recovering *eros*-addicts and individualists who continue to act on the compulsions of insatiable desire (see Gal. 5:17)? The only way we can *avoid* buying into the lie is to practice *yielding* to the Spirit who has come to "**guide us into all the truth**" (John 16:13). Through the Scriptures and corresponding life-labs, the Spirit is eager to expose for us the rationale, schemes, and counterfeits of Worthless's marketplace and effectively cure us of *desiring desire*—"**The Lord is my Shepherd, I shall not want**" (Psa. 23:1).

To gratify his envy and selfish ambition, "the father of the lie" devised a strategy to defeat the true God in the custody battle over human beings by maturing within each of us his own corrupt *eros* nature: "**evil desire** [*desiring desire*] **and greed which is idolatry**" (Col. 3:5). This strategy is a *de-gene-rative* process of fission decay: the corruption of our body by *self-indulgence* (**I want**), leading to the corruption of the soul by *self-will* (**I *will* have**), which leads to the corruption of the human spirit by *self-worth-ship* (**I *deserve* to have**). The love of money (mammon) is the granddaddy of all self-worth-ship; therefore, throughout Worthless's world, both secular and religious, the lines between **economics and worth-ship** (religion) are *very* blurry. Hosea observed:

> [1]*Israel is a **luxuriant vine** [e.g., degenerate, drawing from Worthless's taproot]; **he produces fruit for himself** [eros, self-indulgence], the more his fruit, the more*

altars he made *[self-worth-ship]; the* **richer**
his land [economic success], the better he
made the **sacred pillars** *[a counterfeit*
dwelling place]. ²*Their heart is* **faithless***;*
now they must bear their guilt. The Lord
[Triune-Jealous] will break down their
altars and destroy their sacred pillars. ⁴*...*
With **worthless oaths** *they make covenants*
[opportunists use Agape with hypocrisy to
lure and exploit one another] (Hosea 10:1-
4).

Idolatry involves an exchange: buying into and
sacrificially worth-shipping and serving a god other
than the true, Triune-God. Idols can be a religious
deity (i.e. Artemis, Cali, Krishna, etc.), an admired
self-made man (Fortune 500 CEO, movie star, athlete,
etc.), material things (dream house, cars, trophy wife),
a secular goal (i.e. successful business, first million
before I'm 30, PhD, scientific discovery, etc.), or a
religious goal of self-righteousness from which we
receive an *eros* payoff (admired pastor, missionary,
or philanthropist; model homeschool family; tithing
consistently; memorizing Bible verses, etc.). Worthless
made certain his marketplaces were stocked with an
enormous variety of counterfeits to idolize, offering a
customized snare for each unique individualist.

When we carefully examine idols, we discover a
common denominator—they are all **mediums of
self-worth-ship** and self-actualization.

*⁴¹**At that time the people of Israel made a calf** [gold fashioned into their own ideal self-image: free-grazers] and **brought a sacrifice to the idol** [indirect self-worthship], and were **rejoicing in the works of their hands** [participating in Worthless's economy]. ⁴²**But God turned away** and delivered them up to **serve the host of heaven** [astrology–counterfeit spirituality of the false-father: upward descent]; as it is written in the book of the prophets, "It was **not to Me** [God Most High] that you offered sacrifices forty years in the wilderness, was it, O house of Israel? ⁴³You also took along the **tabernacle of Moloch** [counterfeit of the dwelling place] and the **star of the god Rompha** [counterfeit of "bright morning star": God in Christ; symbol stolen for counterfeit fusion: con-fusion], the images which you made [of dirt] to worship. I also will **remove you** beyond Babylon [exile, fission]" (Acts 7:41-43).*

To construct the golden calf, countless individuals sacrificially contributed their own gold because they had bought into Worthless's lie that this god could gratify their own desire for desire. The gold that they contributed was actually a gift from God who allowed these "slaves" to "plunder the Egyptians" during their exodus (Ex. 12:36). Yet, in expectation of a payoff, these individualists **sold God's gift** and used it to *buy into* another god; they were *investing* in their own self-worth-ship. In the world today, **investing in self-worth-ship** is a trillion-dollar industry. It constitutes such a vast portion of the marketplace that the rest of the economy could not function without.

The essential activity of Worthless's marketplace is investing all our time, energies, and capital in the construction of idols; motivated by *desiring desire*, we chase the mirage of a payoff. Investing in the construction of idols is **exchanging God for self**: "they have forsaken Me [*sold "God is true"*] and have offered sacrifices to other gods, and worshipped the works of their own hands" (Jer. 1:16). Opportunists exploit other human beings to construct, promote and sell expressions of their own self-image. Through Ezekiel, God added:

> *9...I will **repay** [lit. give] you according to your ways [self-indulgence, opportunism], while your abominations are in your midst [idols—self-made mediums of self-worth-ship]; then you will know that I, the Lord do the smiting. 10...the rod has budded, **arrogance has blossomed** [nature of false-father fully mature in man]. 12...Let not the **buyer** rejoice nor the **seller** mourn; for wrath is against all their multitude [participants in Worthless's economy]. 13Indeed, **the seller will not regain** [lit. return to] **what he***

sold [e.g., glory/truth of God eclipsed and lost]…nor will any of them maintain his life [self-preservation] by his iniquity [shrewd, calculated self-interest] (Ezek. 7:9-13).

How, then, does God Most High—three, humble Self-givers—mercifully introduce Their own economy of values, or *worth*, to mature opportunists so deeply acculturated and skilled in Worthless's marketplace?

*[27]**God has chosen the foolish** things of the world [of no value in Worthless's economy] to shame the **wise** [in eros rationale, calculation], and God has **chosen the weak** things of the world to shame the things which are **strong** [predatory opportunists], [28]and **the base things** of the world and the **despised** God has chosen, the things that **are not**, so that He may nullify [bring to futility] the things that **are** [of worth in Worthless's economy], [29]**so that no man may boast** [manifest the self-worth-ship of the false-father] before God [Three who humbly exalt and sacrificially add to One Another] (1 Cor. 1:27-29).*

Tower of Babel Replicated

Worthless designed his marketplace to effectively captivate and snare God's children individually and collectively and hold them hostage in the cosmic custody battle. However, the false-father wove into the fabric and function of the economic system of his world an even **grander scheme**, the *ultimate* plan to gratify his own insatiable desire. The sign of Christ's birth was a **star**—a vortex of atomic nuclear fusion yielding light and life that uniquely represented "the fullness" of the Trinity dwelling in Self-giving Oneness in the Nucleus of the God-Man Jesus (Matt. 2:2-10; Col. 2:9). The **star** symbolized faith, hope, and *Agape* for this promised Messiah, "the **Sunrise** from on high" (Luke 1:78) who would "guide" human beings into Himself. Worthless is an envious usurper, an impostor, and a **counterfeiter**; the symbol which the false-father chose to steal from God, pervert, and use to represent himself and his counterfeit kingdom is a star—a **pentagram**.

The father of the lie is not an innovative creator; he only desires what God desires, except he desires it all *for* himself: "I will **raise** my throne above the stars [*children*] of God, and **I will sit on the mount of assembly** [*kingdom cohabitation*]....I will **ascend** above the heights of the clouds; I will make myself like the Most High" (Isa. 14:13-14). **The tower of Babel** is a profound example of Worthless's own envy and selfish ambition being manifested in human beings **con-fused** to him in his corrupt, *de-gene-rate* likeness. Not only is the false-father the hidden source of man's initial idea to undertake the construction of this city and tower, but he also **covertly provided the blueprints**. First, Worthless breathed into inebriated, dispirited dirt-bags his ancient agenda, making them believe it was their own inspiration; then, he used these unwitting captives to build for him an empire of dirt—**a counterfeit kingdom**—a tower he could stand upon to make himself equal with God:

> [4] *They said, "Come, let us **build for ourselves a city** [cohabitation], and **a tower** whose top will reach into heaven, and let us **make for ourselves a name**, otherwise we [dirt-bags] will be scattered abroad [in fission] over the face of the whole earth."* [5] *The Lord came down to see the city and the tower which the sons of men [corrupt de-gene-rates] had built.* [6] *The Lord said, "Behold, they are **one people** [con-fused in a counterfeit nucleus: the false-father], and they all have the **same language**. And this is what they began to do [Worthless's ancient agenda: envious self-exaltation], and now nothing they purpose to do will be impossible for them.* [7] *Come let **Us** [Father, Son, Spirit–God Most High] go down there and **confuse** their language [de-fuse their con-fusion].... * [8] *So the Lord scattered them abroad [in fission] from there over the face of the whole earth [e.g., to await the true God-Man Nucleus]; and they stopped building the city.* [9] *Therefore its name was called **Babel** [lit. Babylon, **confuse**]"* (Gen. 11:4-9).

The meaning of the con-fusion of Babel goes far beyond mere language; it describes individuals relating to each other in a contrived (artificial) oneness within a counterfeit nucleus. The ancient taproot of Babel, Babylon, and Baal is sun-worship or star-worship—a counterfeit of "Jesus…the bright morning star" (Rev. 22:16). The false-father knows the ultimate aim of God Most High is fusion Oneness with human beings in the Nucleus of the God-Man Jesus—the kingdom of God. In this true cohabitation, "the city which comes down out of heaven from God" (Rev. 3:12), individuals exalt one another, enrich its economy by reciprocal gene-rosity, and freely spend and invest its currency: sacrificial self-giving. Therefore, Worthless's ultimate aim is con-fusion with human beings: counterfeit oneness by mutual exploitation—a kingdom with its own economy and currency: "[15]This is the **exultant city** [cohabitation of sons of Worthless] which dwells securely [self-promotion, self-preservation, and self-indulgence by eros economics], who says in her heart, '*I am, and there is no one besides me* [usurping the place of I AM in self-worth-ship]'" (Zeph. 2:15).

Building this corporate expression of himself—a counterfeit cohabitation, a **monopoly**—is Worthless's cleverly concealed objective and the **driving force of world economics**. A careful examination of the Scriptures reveals that this unclean *spiritual* force is empowering, navigating, and piloting the *natural* marketplace.

*17[And **the beast**] provides that no one will be able to **buy or sell** [participate in Worthless's world economy], except the one who has the mark [identification in the counterfeit nucleus, con-fusion], either the name of the beast or the number of **his name**. 18Here is wisdom. Let him who has understanding [of Worthless's ancient agenda and hidden schemes] calculate the number of the beast, for the number is that of **a man**; and his number is six hundred and sixty-six (Rev. 13:17-18).*

This beast is "a man," but *not* a solitary man; rather, it is a group of predatory opportunists running together in a pack with a shared identity. The father of the lie has made countless attempts to **replicate** God's purpose to fuse all human beings into Christ as "one new man" (Eph. 2:15)—a cohabitation of individuals with one DNA, one Spirit, one name, one mind, and one economy. The expression of *the beast* in the physical world is comprised of individual human beings *con-fused* to Worthless as sharers in his corrupt, de-gene-rate DNA, maturing in him as one man (666) with one name and cohabiting with him in one kingdom with one economy. Jesus said, **"Any kingdom divided against itself is laid waste**; and a house divided against itself **falls**. If Satan also is divided against himself, how will his kingdom stand?" (Luke 11:17-18).

How, then, does the false-father convince corrupt, fiercely independent **individualists** to buy into his fabricated **cohabitation**? Opportunists must find a solution to the famines they repeatedly cause by their own greedy, counter-productive behavior, yet they willfully seek a solution other than losing their lives into the Nucleus of God in Christ. The most difficult thing in the world for an individualist is simply to come to Jesus and lose his life in fusion into Him; the only other alternative is **coming to one another in con-fusion**. I calculate that my chances for self-indulgence and self-preservation are better running together in a pack with others of like mind (*eros rationale*) than on my own. **Predators run in packs**.

The **Nazis** are a notable example of "the beast" seeking an empire of dirt. During a **severe economic depression and famine** in Germany, when mammon "failed" (Luke 16:9), Adolf Hitler rose up on the public stage with answers the people were all too eager to hear. Due to runaway inflation, German currency became so **worthless** that nearly a life's savings was required to buy groceries. Hitler promised abundant prosperity by building one tower under one flag— **the Third Reich with one Fuhrer**—a blasphemous *counterfeit* of the fusion of the Trinity in the Nucleus of Christ, an attempt to *replicate* God's power-source. In desperation, the majority of Germans foolishly bought into Worthless's lie, agenda, and influence manifested in and through Hitler. A many-membered "beast" was created that tyrannized the world and ultimately led Hitler himself to commit suicide. Once Hitler knew he had lost the war, and would inevitably be captured and **brought down** from his Eagle's Nest in humiliation (upward descent) before the world, he shot himself in a consummate act of self-preservation.

From personal experience, David understood the uncertainty and treachery of Worthless's world economy, and he prayed:

> *⁵**My soul** [free will], **wait in silence for God only** [e.g., I will not call other opportunists in the marketplace and join them in confusion], for **my hope** is from Him, ⁶He only is **my rock** and my salvation; **my stronghold** [I invest myself comprehensively into Triune-solidarity], I shall not be **shaken** [when Worthless's economy fails].... ⁹Men of **low degree** are only vanity and **men of rank** [in Worthless's hierarchy] **are a lie** [pretenders, impostors: Worthless's pawns]; in the **balances** [kingdom economy] they go up; they are lighter than breath. ¹⁰**Do not trust in** [buy into] **oppression** and do not vainly hope in robbery [opportunism]; if **riches** increase, do not set your heart upon them [invest in and cherish mammon destined to fail] (Psa. 62:5-10).*

Initially, inebriated, dispirited dirt-bags are not even aware the devil is involved in this counterfeit oneness and plan to build a city and a tower (i.e. business or organizational empire); they believe *themselves* to be the inspiration, architects, and beneficiaries of the scheme. Later, one by one, each of these participants begins to realize he is caught in something much bigger than himself, **the tail is wagging the dog**, and the false-father is revealed. However, by the time a man realizes he is moving in an *upward descent*, Worthless has already **set his barbed-hook**. As a shrewd deceiver, he continues to exploit their insatiable desire compelling them to invest deeper into the lie that they will receive a substantial payoff by **pledging allegiance** to him and joining him as partners. Even by non-religious persons this juncture is literally called **making a deal with the devil**.

For example, a criminal master-mind skillfully recruits a crew of accomplices by making them believe they will each get their individual cut of the take from the robbery. However, since the main thief is usually **shrewder** than his companions, at the most vulnerable moment during their get-away or when they are no longer useful to him, he will abandon and betray them in order to keep it all for himself.

The land of the Canaanites, where God planted and tested Israel, was full of shrines on high places—"**the high places of Baal** [*sun-god*]" (Num. 22:41; Deut. 12:2)—unmistakable evidence that the inhabitants were in con-fusion with Worthless, manifesting his ancient, envious desire, and participating in his economy. Rather than obeying God's command to tear down these high places and destroy the economic system that inspired their construction, Israel *sold* God Most High in order to *buy into* this **counterfeit worth-ship**, and it became a bitter and addictive snare through all the centuries the people of Israel lived in that land. There are more than 100 references that cite "the high places" as the specific reason Israel continually stumbled and suffered estrangement and exile from God Most High (1 Kings 3:3; 2 Kings 23:13; 2 Chron. 15:17).

The taproot of Worthless's own **king of the mountain** motivation and agenda is evident in secular business today, but it is far more toxic and ugly in the unsanctified church. In the capital city of Ukraine, Kiev, there is a war memorial monument on a prominent hill top—a woman constructed of titanium holding a sword in the air. When the Eastern Orthodox Church discovered that her sword reached an **elevation** higher than the topmost spire of their prominent cathedral, they raised hell! Now the woman is literally holding up a knife! God spoke through Jeremiah:

> *[1] The **lofty stronghold** has been put to shame; it has been captured...and shattered [upward descent].... [7] For because of your **trust in your own achievements and treasures** [opportunism, economic success], even you yourself will be captured.... [18] **Come down***

from your glory [self-exaltation] *and sit in thirst* [self-emptied] *on the **parched ground** [in the dust; e.g., return to reality].... ²⁹We have heard of the pride of Moab—he is very proud—of his haughtiness, his pride, his arrogance and his **self-exaltation.** ³⁰"I know his **fury**," declares the Lord, "but it is futile; his idle boasts have accomplished nothing...."*

*²"For behold, I have made you **small** among the nations, **despised** [worthless] among men.*

*¹⁶As for the terror of you, the **arrogance** of your heart [self-worth-ship – "the lie"] has **deceived** you, O you who live in the clefts of the rock [self-preservation], who **occupy the height** of the hill [self-exaltation]. Though you make your nest as **high** as an eagle's [i.e. Hitler's Eagles Nest], I will bring you **down** from there," declares the Lord (Jer. 48:1-30; Obad. 2; Jer. 49:16).*

The economy of Worthless's world is a **direct reflection** and expression of his own corrupt, *de-gene-rate* nature as an envious usurper and opportunist; the marketplace is a **hierarchy**, a pyramid scheme illustrated by the Tower of Babel. The false-father himself—"the god of this world who has blinded the minds of the unbelieving" (2 Cor. 4:4)—sits upon the **pinnacle** of this pyramid as its concealed and mysterious figurehead.

The European Union is a profound illustration of Worthless's **direct influence** upon the design and practical operation of world economies. In its formative days, the European Union developed a **promotional poster**; the chosen artwork is a painting by Brueghel (1563) literally entitled "**The Tower of Babel**." The motto beneath reads, "**Europe: Many Tongues, One Voice**." Curiously, the architectural design of the European Union Parliament Building located in Strasbourg, France bears a remarkable resemblance to Brueghel's depiction of the Tower of Babel. Further, the image of **Europa riding on a beast** is depicted in large, metal sculptures in front of certain facilities of the European Union as well as on postage stamps and certain coins of EU currency. This scantily-clad woman riding on a beast bears an unmistakable likeness to a scene in John's Revelation:

> [3]...I saw a **woman sitting on a scarlet beast,** full of blasphemous names, having seven heads and ten horns. [4]The woman was clothed in purple and scarlet, and adorned with **gold** and **precious stones** and **pearls** [symbols of economic success], having in her hand a **gold cup full of abominations** and of the unclean things of her immorality, [5]and on her forehead a name

*was written, a mystery, "**BABYLON** THE*
GREAT [cohabitation of con-fusion], THE
MOTHER OF HARLOTS [opportunists]
AND OF THE ABOMINATIONS OF
THE EARTH" (Rev. 17:3-5).

It is not merely the economic infrastructure of the European Union that Worthless inspires, shapes, and manipulates but also the interdependent economies of the entire world. Is it a coincidence that the dynamic forces of the **stock exchange** are depicted by a bull and a bear—two predatory beasts in tension with one another? One man observed, "The market is weird. Every time one guy sells, another one buys, and they both think they're smart."

In the world economy, **resources flow up** from the have-nots to elite opportunists seeking to gratify their insatiable desire by shrewd calculation, deception, and applied force of threat when necessary—exploiting those beneath them in the crab bucket either by false promises or oppression. In the marketplace, when an employee is fired, typically the stressful job of informing that worker is conveniently delegated to a floor manager who, with self-protecting indifference, says something like, "**This decision came down from the top**." As a reactionary measure, workers' unions are formed, but like Frankenstein's monster, they become corrupted from within and give birth to new elite opportunists in place of old ones. All these **power brokers** cannot see that they *themselves* are **pawns** in

Worthless's ancient scheme—used to preserve and perpetuate the hierarchy the false-father established among his captives. "Professing to be wise, they became fools" (Rom. 1:22).

In the economy of the kingdom, **resources flow down** from above, sacrificing lifting and raising the needy and filling and enriching the empty. "Every good thing given and every perfect gift is **from above, coming down from the Father** of lights [*lit. luminaries: Father of created beings abiding in fusion with Him*], with whom there is no variation [*eros-free*] or shifting shadow [*Agape without hypocrisy*]" (James 1:17). Through the prophet Habakkuk, God exposed the influence that Worthless's ancient agenda has upon the **economic objectives** of mankind:

> [9]Woe to him who **gets evil gain for his house** [*opportunism*], **to put his nest on high [self-exaltation]**, to be delivered from the hand of calamity [*self-preservation*]! [10]You have devised a shameful thing for your house, by cutting off many peoples [*e.g., in the crab bucket*]; so you are **sinning against yourself** [*hastening de-gene-rative fission decay: an upward descent*]. [11]Surely **the stone will cry out from the wall**, and the rafter will answer it from the framework [*individual human beings–living stones– forced into a counterfeit dwelling place and exploited*].

> ^{12}Woe to him who **builds a city** [an empire of dirt] **with bloodshed** and founds a town with violence [coercive authority]! ^{13}Is it not indeed from the **Lord of hosts** [Nucleus of individuals fused by Agape] that peoples toil for fire, and **nations grow weary** [in Worthless hard-labor camp] **for nothing?** [In mercy, God permits futility and famine to bring opportunists to the end of themselves.] ^{14}For the earth will be **filled with the glory of the Lord** [human beings fused into the Nucleus of the Most High], as the waters cover **the sea** [e.g., sea of humanity] (Hab. 2:9-14).

Replications of the tower of Babel (counterfeit dwelling place) are destined to **fall** because they are erected by individualists compelled by insatiable desire in con-fusion (counterfeit fusion), **climbing** on one another in self-exaltation. Limited resources soon run out among these predatory opportunists, and there is nothing left but to bite, devour, and consume one another. The lofty and exalted dwelling place of the kingdom of God **comes down** to us in Christ, in *downward ascent*; this true cohabitation is established among men *not* by pride and individualism but by humble, fuse-able individuals who sacrificially **lift one another up by practicing kingdom economics**:

*[11]And He [God in Christ] gave some as apostles, and some as prophets, and some as evangelists, and some as pastors and teachers [unique individuals], [12]for the equipping of the saints for **the work of service** [serving one another: kingdom economics] to the **building up** of the [many-membered] body of Christ; [13]until we attain to the **unity of the faith** [re-gene-ration in one fuse-able DNA], and of the knowledge of the Son of God [Nucleus of the Most High], to a **mature man** [many-membered man perfected in Trinity-like Oneness], to the **measure of the stature** [height] which belongs to the **fullness** of Christ [the combined and combining God-Man].... [15]But speaking the truth in Agape, we are to **grow up** in all aspects into Him [God-Man Nucleus] who is the head, even Christ, [16]from whom the whole body, being **fitted and joined** [fused] **together by what every joint supplies** [reciprocal gene-rosity: sacrificial self-giving/sharing], according to the proper working of each individual part [e.g., according to the relational blueprints of the Trinity] causes the **growth** of the body [mutual-indwelling place] for the **building of itself up in Agape** (Eph. 4:11-16).*

Famine and Bounty

As we previously observed, the economy of the world is a **consumer-driven** operation—a counterproductive exercise of takers that results in lack. Our *de-gene-rate* instinct as individualists— *desiring desire*, self-indulgence, self-preservation, and fear of scarcity and loss—precipitates a free-fall into **famine** and a war-like state in which the *predatory* behavior of opportunism matures. The economy of the kingdom is a **producer-driven** operation—a fruit-bearing exercise of givers that *gene-rates* superabundant **bounty**. Free individuals who participate in the dynamic of *reciprocal gene-rosity*—sacrificial self-sharing and self-giving—facilitate a cohabitation of peace in which resources are exponentially multiplied and *gene-rous* behavior matures.

Through deception, the father of the lie captured both Adam and the stewardship over the earth that God had *entrusted* to Adam. As an impostor, usurper, and individualist, Worthless *claims* to be the **sole proprietor** of the world, but he does *not* own the world. Ownership belongs to God; more precisely, the whole creation is held in trust on our behalf by **three incorruptible Trustees**, Father, Son, and Spirit as "fellow heirs with Christ" (Rom. 8:17). "Behold, to the Lord your God belong heaven and the highest heavens, the earth and **all that is in it**" (Deut. 10:13).

In the *de-gene-rate* likeness of the false-father, human beings continually **abuse God's creation** by seeking to *acquire*, *possess*, and *control* it as an empire of dirt:

> [10]*Many shepherds have **ruined** My vineyard [abusing stewarded authority], they have **trampled down** My field [creation], they have made My pleasant field [intended to provide bounty] a **desolate wilderness.** [11]...Desolate it mourns before Me; the whole land has been made desolate because **no man lays it** [kingdom economics: reciprocal gene-rosity] **to heart.** [12]On all the bare heights [lit. caravan trails; e.g., of traders] in the wilderness, **destroyers** have come.... There is **no peace for anyone** [in Worthless's marketplace]. [13]They have sown wheat and have **reaped thorns;** they have strained themselves to **no profit** [their futile nature and behavior reaps futile circumstances: famine]. But **be ashamed of your harvest** [lit. products]...* (Jer. 12:10-13).

We cause **famines** then blame it on God and one another. Yet, in compassion, humility, and altruism (*Agape*), the Triune-Most High *condescends* to **serve** all of us beastly individualists, **feeding** us out of Their own *gene-rative*, relational fullness:

> [9]*You visit the earth and cause it to **overflow** [by Your gene-rous, bountiful Presence]; You*

*greatly **enrich** it; the **stream of God** [Three flowing together] is **full** of water ["fullness" pouring out on the earth]. You **prepare their grain** [feed beasts by sacrificial Self-giving], for thus You **prepare** the earth [as three servant-hearted Stewards]. [10] You water its furrows **abundantly**, You settle its ridges, You soften it with showers, You bless its **growth**. [11] You have crowned the year with **Your bounty** [superabundant yield of Triune-Agape], and Your paths drip with fatness (Psa. 65:9-11).*

The life of *de-gene-rate*, *eros*-infected human beings is a strange paradox: we instinctively practice the predatory ways of the **false-father** that inevitably result in futility and famine, yet at the end of the day, it is our **true Father** who actually feeds us: "The **young lions** do lack and **suffer hunger** [*famine*].... The **young lions roar after their prey and seek their food from God**" (Psa. 34:10; 104:21). Apart from *re-gene-ration* in the divine nature of Agape, however, it is impossible for to receive, cherish, share, and reciprocate God's bounty: "**Is your eye envious because I AM generous?**" (Matt. 20:15). As David saw forward to Christ, bought into Him, and became acculturated into the economy of the Most High, he reflected upon the torturous history of his suspicious and wayward people who abused God's superabundant *gene-rosity*:

*⁸A stubborn and rebellious [self-willed] generation...whose **spirit was not faithful to God** [idolatry of self-worth-ship].... ¹⁰They did not keep the covenant of God [fusion agreement], and refused to walk in His law [reciprocal Agape: kingdom economics]; ¹¹they **forgot** His deeds [gene-rosity], and His miracles that He had shown them. ¹⁵...**He split the rock** [type of Christ: Triune-Solidarity] in the wilderness, and [sacrificially] gave them **abundant drink** like the ocean depths. ¹⁷... Yet they still continued to sin against Him, to rebel against the Most High in the desert. ¹⁸And in their heart they **put God to the test [suspicion] by asking food according to their desire** [desiring desire; self-indulgence]. ¹⁹Then they spoke against God; they said, "Can God prepare a table in the wilderness? ²⁰Behold, He struck the rock so that the waters gushed out, and streams were overflowing; **can He give bread also?** Will He provide meat for His people?*

*²¹Therefore the Lord heard and was full of wrath... ²²because they **did not believe in God** [Three true to One Another and to us] **and trust in** [buy into] His salvation. ²³Yet He commanded the clouds above and opened the doors of heaven... ²⁴and gave them **food from heaven** [type of Christ:*

Bread from heaven]. *[25]...He sent them food in abundance... [26]round about their dwellings. [29]So they ate and were well filled, and* **their desire He gave to them***. [30]Before they had satisfied their* **desire***, while the food was still in their mouths, [31]the anger of God rose against them and killed some of their stoutest ones [individualists] and* **subdued** *[lit. caused to bow down] the choice men of Israel. [32]In spite of all this [superabundant Agape] they still sinned [eros addiction] and did not believe in [buy into] His wonderful works. [33]So He brought their days to an end in* **futility***....*

[34]When He killed them, they sought Him, and returned and searched diligently for God; [35]and they **remembered that God was their rock** *[Triune-solidarity],* **and the Most High** *[Three exalting One Another]* **their Redeemer.** *[36]But they* **deceived** *Him with their mouth, and* **lied** *to Him with their tongue [Agape with hypocrisy]. [37]For their heart was not steadfast [true] toward Him. [41]...Again and again they tempted God, and* **pained** *the Holy One of Israel (Psa. 78:8-41).*

Due to our own *insatiable desire,* and buying and selling one another for personal gain, we bring **famine** upon ourselves and then call our predicament an act of God. Even while chewing the food God has provided in **relief-aid**, we are simultaneously blaming Him for our circumstances! Father sent us to live in Uganda, East Africa so we would recognize this same grievous response of **ingratitude** and **entitlement,** as it often appears in more sophisticated forms in all other nations. Acculturated into Worthless's rationale and economy, we do not share the Triune-God's economy of worth. Through the prophet Haggai, God made clear why this doesn't work:

> [5]*"Consider your ways! [6]You [individualists] have **sown much** [in Worthless's labor-camp], but **harvest little** [famine]; you eat, but there is **not enough** to be satisfied; you drink, but there is not enough to become drunk; you put on clothing, but no one is warm enough; and he who earns, earns wages to put into **a purse with holes** [e.g., a purse given to you by a thief!]."*

> [7]*Thus says the **Lord of hosts** [Nucleus of multitudes of unique individuals in fusion], "Consider your [corrupt, futile] ways! [8]**Go up to the mountains** [e.g., seek God Most High], bring wood [e.g., heavenly resources] and **rebuild the temple** [lit. house; true treasure: cohabitation of reciprocal gene-rosity], that I may be pleased with it and*

be glorified," says the Lord. ⁹"You look for **much***, but behold, it comes to* **little***; when you bring it home, I blow it away.* **Why?***" declares the Lord of hosts, "because of* **My house** *which lies desolate, while each of you runs to* **his own house** *[fission in individualism: self-worth-ship]. ¹⁰Therefore, because of you [dispirited dirt-bags] the sky has withheld its dew and the earth has withheld its produce" (Haggai 1:5-10).*

Once the Spirit helps me to *sober up* and awaken to the economy of God Most High, even when I am in circumstances of scarcity and need, I feel wealthier and far more secure than those who have accumulated vast resources in this uncertain, treacherous world. John testified, "We know that we are **of God** [*invested into the Rock–Triune-Most High*], and that the whole world [*economy*] **lies in the power of the evil one** [*the treacherous false-father Worthless*]" (1 John 5:19). See how Paul *overcame* the power of mammon and *transcended* Worthless's world economy by faith in (*buying into*) the economy of God Most High:

> *¹¹...I have learned to be* **content** *[at rest, free from anxiety] in whatever circumstances I am [in Worthless's world]. ¹²I know how to get along with* **humble means***, and I also know how to live in* **prosperity** *[in the world economy, famine and abundance are*

temporal illusions, earthly mirages]; in any and every circumstance **I have learned the secret of** *being filled and going hungry, both of having* **abundance** *and suffering* **need** *[e.g., I move with God in downward ascent].* [13]*I can do all things [any act of self-denial or sacrificial self-giving needed]* **through Him** *[God in Christ] who strengthens me [with fusion power]* (Phil. 4:11-13).

In the next *Plumbline, God Magnified Part Seven: Surveying the Economy of the Kingdom,* we will see how "Jesus, Son of the Most High God" (Luke 8:28) came down to us in our "fallen" state, to mentor us in **kingdom economics** that we might become "**sons** [*and daughters*] **of the Most High**" (Luke 6:35).

God Magnified Series

Part 1: Discovering the "Us" in Oneness

A journey of progressive magnification of the worth-ship of God by meditating on five of the fourteen "God is" statements in Scripture. These statements are like porch pillars of the eternal dwelling place that the Trinity share in perpetual fusion Oneness in *Agape*. The Triune-God intentionally left Their spiritual fingerprint in the powersource of the natural universe—atomic nuclear fusion—"God is a sun."

Part 2: Exploring the Dwelling Place

Our journey continues around the porch pillars of the eternal dwelling place of Light in which the Father, Son, and Spirit indwell One Another in fusion Oneness. Eric leads us through a clear understanding of "God is Light" and "God is a sun and shield" explaining the vortex of the Trinity and how we are called to be sharers of their holiness and mature children of Light.

Part 3: Revealing the Secret of the Mystery

This volume focuses on Pillar 8, "God in Christ," where we discover the secret mystery of our participation in the dynamic of the kingdom—the fusion of the Triune-God and regenerated sons and daughters dwelling together in the God-Man Jesus.

Part 4: Awakening to Spiritual Reality

This volume focuses on Pillar 9, "God is Spirit," where we discover how Father, Son, and Spirit fuse into One Another as a whirlwind. The Triune-Spirit created individual human beings as a tri-unity—spirit, soul, and body. We will learn how as free individuals we are fused by *Agape* into the Triune-Spirit.

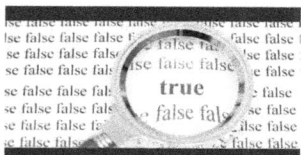

Part 5: Discerning "The Truth"

This volume focuses on Pillar 10, "God is true," revealing a deeper understanding of the divine nature of *Agape*—the "true" Love by which Father, Son, and Spirit abide in perpetual fusion as one God. We will discover how truth is in Jesus and how we by His grace becomes sharers of that truth. By carefully examining and receiving this truth, which the Triune-God desires to plant, cultivate, and mature within us, we are made capable of participating in a relationship of reciprocal generosity with Father, Son, Spirit and one another —the kingdom of God.

LIFECHANGERS®

P.O. Box 3709 ❖ Cookeville, TN 38502
931.520.3730 ❖ lc@lifechangers.org

www.ingramcontent.com/pod-product-compliance
Lightning Source LLC
Chambersburg PA
CBHW061745020426
42331CB00006B/1362